Advanced Praise for
*Humility: The Key to Greatness*

Bill Grimbol, with lightning speed, digs deep into questions of what gives our lives meaning and purpose — all in the context of an entertaining conversation between two friends who have dispensed with idle chit-chat. *Humility: The Key to Greatness* recalls the classic film *My Dinner with Andre* and delivers a meaningful and welcome gut punch on life and how we choose to live it.

Neils Mueller
Writer/Director, *The Assassination of Richard Nixon*, *Small Town Wisconsin*

When two men in their seventies, former boyhood friends, asked themselves—Are we pursuing a way of life which will enable us to leave a legacy of significance—*Humility: The Key to Greatness*, by Bill Grimbol, seeks to answer their question. Through Grimbol's deeply personal memories and insights from his dear friend, Manuel Barrera, Jr., this fine volume discusses an American ethos rarely seen today. The book makes a strong case for striving toward humility which this reader found both challenging and compelling.

Jeff Neubauer
Executive Director
Higher Expectations for Racine County

*Humility: The Key to Greatness* is a tender and meaningful testament to the lifelong friendship of two beautiful souls, Bill Grimbol and Manuel Barrera, Jr. From school days onward, they sought answers to many of life's deepest questions. Their final conversations on living a life of value that results in an honorable legacy made me reexamine my own life. Couldn't I be more grateful, mindful, accepting, and inclusive?

Nancy Neider

# Humility: The Key to Greatness

Rev. William R. Grimbol

With excerpts written by Manuel Barrera, Jr., Ph.D.

www.ten16press.com - Waukesha, WI

Humility: The Key to Greatness
Copyrighted © 2022 Rev. William R. Grimbol
ISBN 9781645383710
First Edition

Humility: The Key to Greatness
by Rev. William R. Grimbol
with excerpts written by Manuel Barrera, Jr., Ph.D.

All Rights Reserved. Written permission must be secured from the publisher to use or reproduce any part of this book, except for brief quotations in critical reviews or articles.

For information, please contact:

www.ten16press.com
Waukesha, WI

Cover design by Kaeley Dunteman

The author has made every effort to ensure that the information within this book was accurate at the time of publication. The author does not assume and hereby disclaims any liability to any party for any loss, damage, or disruption caused by errors or omissions, whether such errors or omissions result from accident, negligence, or any other cause.

This book is dedicated to
Lea Barrera and Justin Grimbol,
in hopes they create their own significant legacies
and carry on what they deem worthy from their fathers.

# THE FOREWORD

## A True Story of a Dream

This is a story of two old friends reconnecting. We first met at Washington Junior High School in Racine, WI. When we came together again, our relationship seemed much the same as in our youth: we spoke a lot, swapped news, ideas, feelings, and dreams. Technology had changed, but we still used the phone to set up plans. One significant thing was missing. We had been active athletes. Football, basketball, baseball, tennis, and golf were relegated to our memory shelves; our bodies would no longer cooperate.

On the eve of my 70th birthday, I received a call from Manuel Barrera, Jr.. We dove into catching up, but then our conversation jetted off on a wild tangent, which happened frequently, and we began discussing the question: "What would you like to be remembered for and what would you hope they would choose to forget?" An embryonic dream formed. Together, we could write a book about our ideas on the concept of LEGACY.

For seven months we shared weekly calls and e-mails. We sought to piece together not only our ideas about LEGACY, but how our childhoods and adolescences had shaped and formed many of our values and beliefs.

Manuel had multiple sclerosis, MS, for forty years and did not view it as a blessing or a curse. To Manuel, fighting was a waste of time and energy, and even love. He received each day as it came, seeking to be as brave, creative, and kind as he could be in response. His humility was deeply rooted in his belief that he was not above or beyond anything life might send his way. Then tragedy stuck, as it so often does. Out of nowhere. Out of everywhere. After forty years of bravely battling and befriending MS, Manuel had a severe exacerbation of the disease, and died on March 20, 2020.

No matter how prepared we think we might be, every death comes with some degree of painful shock. Regarding our project, I felt like everything was shattered on the floor, like the pieces of Popeye after a wallop from Brutus. I was left holding the proverbial bag from our dream, a bag with seven months of notes on our discussions, thoughts, ideas, and anecdotes, plus a strong outline. It's fascinating to see how many seeds for this manuscript were planted long ago. Ironically, Manuel's rough draft of a first chapter arrived the same day I learned of his death. We had intended to write the chapters back and forth. With Manuel's death, neither the back nor the forth were possible any longer.

Wincing with moist eyes, I decided to go it alone. It felt important to share the story, or at least the journey up until the point of Manuel's passing. I thought he would respect my choice, as I do not recall him ever quitting anything.

So, I will do my utmost to recapture the true spirit of our wonderful talks, and the hope, purpose, and meaning they captured in us both. Manuel did not want our book to feel like a combined memoir. We wanted to share our ideas on the concept of LEGACY and I am trying to honor that mission.

The process of preparing to write the book was like a spiritual game of tennis. The ball was the idea. The strokes were never a slam. There were no aces. This was just a relaxed lobbing game for the fun of it, and only rarely was there a sharply hit backhand, or a spinning serve, intended to make an important point. Nobody kept score, and if we had, even after so many hours of play, the score would have remained love-love.

It is an amazing gift to write a book with a great friend and a truly great man. It was an honor to share stories, ideas, hopes and dreams in our early seventies. I so wish we had gotten the chance to complete the book together, but we did not. Like so much of life, the dream was deferred, or maybe in this case, more accurately, the dream had morphed.

This book carries my strong wish to pay tribute to Manuel, as it should. He hated the spotlight, but he has no say in the matter, other than offering a scowling curse from somewhere above. Even from beyond the blue, I can hear his voice and I know he wants the core of the manuscript to remain true to the lessons we felt deserved passing on. Each lesson highlights an aspect of the true spirit of creating a genuinely good life—a life capable of greatness.

We both were concerned and saddened by the present state of our culture, which talks endlessly of a good life while offering only a lifestyle with little to nothing to do with doing or being good. If anything, Manuel and I wanted a return to the basics of goodness. We wanted to strongly advocate for a kinder, more compassionate, merciful, and unconditionally loving culture. A culture which celebrated equality and diversity—just like the creation itself.

We also hoped to celebrate the tips, hints, and wisdom we learned growing up in Racine, Wisconsin, even during the infamous '60s. We also wished to pass on the values planted by our families, friends, and our hometown.

The best way for me to pay tribute to Manuel, is to write this book on my own. I promise him, myself, and his family, that I will strive for an accurate reflection of our legacy lessons from seven months of phone calls and letters.

I approach this as I did writing hundreds of eulogies during forty plus years as a pastor, as a chance to lift up the best of someone, the qualities which made them unforgettable. The only difference is that this time I am writing not just about an individual I respected, cherished, and loved, but also a friendship which utterly transformed my life.

One final comment before we officially begin. Manuel was a truly great man, an authentically great man. His greatness would become the incessant commentary on his own legacy. His greatness was grounded in humility. That humility validated his greatness, expressed his modest ambitions, and became the essence of how he would be remembered.

In this crazily vain and arrogant culture of celebrity we live in, please pay attention to a life of true greatness, one carved out of a substantial amount of genuine humility. Take notice. It is a real gift—as was Manuel.

# Lesson One:

# NOTICE WHAT MATTERS

"Listen to your life. See it for the fathomless mystery that it is. In the boredom and pain of it, no less than in the excitement and gladness: touch, taste, smell your way to the holy hidden heart of it, because in the last analysis all moments are key moments, and life itself is grace."
–Frederick Buechner

"The things that matter most must never be at the mercy of the things that matter least."
–Goethe

In our conversations, Manuel and I found a common thread: what impact had we made in our respective lines of work? We both questioned if we had made any great strides, or significant difference, but did admit to believing we had touched lives in positive and productive ways.

Manuel asked some significant questions. "Were there any moments when you felt like you had failed, or were just not reaching the people you hoped to be serving? Did you wonder what was missing in what you were doing? I guess, what I am asking, is when you did hit bottom professionally, which I assume you did, now and then, what was it you were questioning, or even mourning?"

I thought for a while, and then surprised myself by my answer.

"I think as a minister, I was consistently stunned by how many adults and youth sought my counsel, or mercy, or affirmation. Yet when I asked them a basic question, to tell me what they were feeling or thinking at this point in their lives, or what they saw as their top priorities, they would stare at me blankly—most did not have a clue. I felt like I was hosting a first meeting of Mutes Anonymous.

"I am sincere, Manuel; so many folks seem completely detached from their inner or spiritual world. I'm not sure where they are, or what they are doing there, but they don't seem all that aware or awake. Their souls haven't been sold, necessarily, but they seem as dry as dust. In a stiff wind, their souls would disappear altogether.

"These are people who have spent one hell of a lot of time in Church, and yet, seem to have no real spiritual life to speak of. No devotional time. Few efforts at service. Most of all, a lack of contact with a Higher Power—or having a Higher Power with any actual power."

Manuel then thought for a while. His response was deep, clear, and sincere.

"I think that could describe me. We're all just so busy, that we have little time to reflect or wonder or examine much of anything. One thing about academia, there's just so much crap work to get done, it's easy to lose sight of the real purpose and point of what we are trying to teach.

"I've attended more meetings than I can count, few of which accomplished anything—other than pure unadulterated repetition. I would much rather have had good talks with my students, than have had to grade or read papers, or give exams which rarely told me anything I did not already know. Every teacher knows their motivated students, as well as those who, for whatever reason, could care less.

"I would bet a good pep talk would have done a lot more for many of my students, rather than telling the teacher what it is that same teacher supposedly taught them."

"Well, since we're being honest here. I have spent most of my life trying to be perfect, being a full-blown people pleaser, and performing on an incessant and usually artificial basis," I added.

"I think you are being a little tough on yourself."

"Well, that is the pot calling the kettle black," I said.

"Okay. Got me there. I do know what you're saying Bill; we are busy doing things about which we either do not care much about, or question the value of . . . correct?"

"Bingo!" I replied.

Manuel had a quick response. "In terms of academia, I think we were asked to spend an inordinate amount of time on matters which simply do not matter. We are still ranked by our peers by what we publish, rather than whether or not we are a good teacher. We are still held accountable for the grades our students earn, whereas, a "C" student may have done far more actual learning, than the "A" student, who just knew how to take an exam, or regurgitate the material."

In response I said, "In the Church, we waste so damn much time on silly protocol, debating our beliefs, and trying to act certain 'our spiritual team' has the right answers—in first place in the numbers game. We are not only lousy at asking questions, or raising doubts, but we are terrified of our youth wondering why we bother with faith in the first place.

Truth be told, we are frequently offering answers to questions nobody is asking," I concluded.

"Ouch!" Manuel said, then laughed. "That hits too close to home. So, what do you suggest we do about it?"

"I would suggest we start paying more attention to what really matters."

"I agree with you Bill, I do, but we are afraid to talk about what really matters, let alone teach it or preach it, because we cannot grade it, or say who has the best ideas, or the worst for that matter. I think academia is just plain afraid to talk about Life, or what we think or feel or experience. It's too mysterious and out of our control."

"Ironically," I replied, "it's ditto for the Church. What matters, which is supposedly our strong suit, is not often discussed, and we keep obsessing over doctrine and dogmas and creeds, in which we find little comfort, challenge, or inspiration.

"Why are we so frightened of not talking about Jesus all the time, or exploring other religions, or looking into what the poets or philosophers, novelists, playwrights, or even scientists have to say? Why does the Church have the crazy notion we must explain away science—a subject in which most clergy have little training, and a genuine need for substantial learning?"

"So, let's talk next time about what we think matters and how we might encourage and enhance our ability to pay attention to those areas?" Manuel suggested.

"Oh . . . just a short casual conversation," I teased.

"Bill, you are the one who needs ten minutes just to say hello . . . remember?"

"Too true. Talk to you at the end of the week."

Manuel persisted. "I would be really pleased if we could come up with a good solid list of what we felt truly mattered in life and to what we hoped our readers would pay greater attention. I see such lessons as our potential legacy. We can pass on what we consider our wisdom. Everyone can, from every level of education or intellect."

"Good point, a legacy does not require being a Rev. or having a Ph.D."

"No . . . every single human being on the planet has something worth saying and something worth hearing."

"This is why our stories matter so much, and why it is so critical to get our children and youth away from gazing at screens in a stupor," I said.

"We can only pass on what we have known with our hearts. We have to experience it, fully, and honestly, to believe it is worthy to share."

"I look forward to our talk."

Neither of us knew this conversational focus would last a full seven months or that it would be abruptly cut short. What follows will be my best effort to capture the spirit and focus of those conversations. Two old friends, trying to figure out how they might be remembered. Two guys getting older and needing to find some meaning to their mornings.

It did not feel daunting or pathetic. It felt right and important.

We looked forward to every conversation. It felt wonderfully awake and alive.

## PAYING ATTENTION TO WHAT MATTERS

Manuel and I were very different people. Our personalities were almost direct opposites. Manuel was quiet, reserved, humble, and intellectually brilliant. I, on the other hand, am a motor mouth, a showboat, have an ego the size of Utah, but happen to think and talk well on my feet.

Both of us were struck with how quickly we put together the list of our ultimate concerns or our top priorities, and what we would encourage others to see as meaningful—maybe even critical—subjects, worthy of our attention.

This list was put together in two, hour-long conversations, and we were pleased to see how the foundation of our friendship was built upon some sturdy rocks of shared values, even though during high school and college we held heated debates on religion and life's meaning. These battles could go on and on, with no debate winner declared. Our beliefs were no longer religious in nature, but more about poetry and philosophy, and offered a spiritual perspective.

Here is the list we composed, a summation of what we felt the human race must embrace as critical and vital to the quality, and yes, the quantity of our lives.

I wish I could literally sound more like Manuel in this section. I don't do impressions, but I can accurately state those concerns and causes we both valued a great deal—and cared passionately about.

## 1. <u>SAVE THE PLANET</u>

What matters is our planet, as we are literally nothing without it.

We both felt strong admiration for the "green movement," and the attention our youth were paying to addressing climate change while coping with the wild weather and a "new normal" in storms, floods, and wildfires.

Our greatest concern was how we adults tended to talk a good line but resisted the changes and **sacrifices** which needed to be made. We shared a concern that capitalism was not good for the earth—especially long term. The price we pay for our standard of living appears to be a fast track to extinction.

The earth is ceaselessly "shouting" about the vital importance of interdependence, cooperation, and sharing. The sad fact is, the last time many of us really talked about the importance of sharing—**was in kindergarten!**

## 2. NURTURE THE SOUL

Both of us were no longer "big" on religion. We were not anti-religion, but felt it had become a system which discouraged people from questioning, doubting, thinking, being scientific, or expressing oneself in the arts.

We had no use for one-size-fits-all religion and struggled with many of the mandatory beliefs espoused by the various forms of organized religion.

We both felt strongly about spirituality, or more importantly, spiritual growth. Manuel liked my contention that spirituality and maturity were pretty much one and the same. We both believed strongly in the presence of a soul, and saw it as the "home" to our ultimate concerns, longings, and deepest convictions.

Nurturing the soul, for us, meant growing in compassion, generosity, graciousness, mercy, and the rigorous pursuit of honesty, justice, and peace. These are sadly nowhere near the top of our cultural priorities; priorities which, unfortunately, turn out shallow seekers of success and acquirers of stuff, who never fully grow up.

## 3. **HAVE AN INFORMED HEART**

Manuel always felt this category was my strong suit. He only thought that because I wore my heart on my sleeve.

I felt he had deep insight, sensitivity, and a most well-informed heart, but his style was far less aggressive or assertive than mine.

Whatever the case, we both believed in having a thoughtful, tender, trustworthy heart, and how vital this was to leading a genuinely good life.

Love is dependent on intimacy. Intimacy is dependent on communication. What we need to talk about are the matters of the heart. This remains the key to a good marriage, good parenting, good friendship, and even being a good citizen.

An informed heart bleeds for others, pays attention to their pains, is kind and sensitive, patient and persevering, and above all else, willing to forgive on a daily basis.

Compassion will prove to be the most important quality of character within the modern man or woman.

## 4. **PRACTICE ACCEPTANCE**

We both saw ACCEPTANCE as an attribute which came with age. We deeply lamented how our culture encouraged us to do battle with life, and how so many folks had transformed life into an endurance test nobody can pass.

We also bore witness to our culture's horrid relationship to time. We kill time. We waste time. We think we can make time. We spend time. Seldom, are we willing to simply accept and receive the gift of the day.

Acceptance is the awareness we are not in control. It is knowing we are not in charge. It is surrendering to a Higher Power, as we understand it. Acceptance is often tolerance, mercy magnified, and a willingness to embrace the notion of being fully human.

We live. We die. We must live while knowing we will die. This requires great courage. It also requires a high degree of trust and acceptance.

Manuel and I came to the conclusion that acceptance would help Americans lower their expectations when it came to money and material goods but raise them for intimacy and love. Down deep, in our bones and hearts, we know what matters, and it is never stuff or numbers, it is our lives and those we love.

## 5. LISTEN TO YOUR BODY OF KNOWLEDGE

The human body is a miracle. It is incessantly informing and guiding us on what we need, to be healthy, happy, and hope-filled. The body speaks in a language of sighs, stress, exhaustion, anxiety, and fear, as well as in awe, wonder, lumps in the throat, and goosebumps. We need to listen to our bodies, hear the lessons being delivered, as well as the warnings and callings being issued.

Manuel had MS for over 40 years, until the day he died from its complications. He never stopped seeing his body as sacred, nor did he ever cease his efforts to understand and befriend his disease. He did not battle MS. He sought to be smarter than MS. He paid diligent attention to what triggered or relieved his symptoms. He begrudgingly but wisely accepted its presence in his life.

In truth, Manuel figured out he had MS, long before the medical community affirmed his suspicions. He paid close attention to his body's wisdom.

My body has had to deal repeatedly with my hoarseness and vocal nodules. I attribute this to my soul screaming for me to get my eating, my exercising, and my resting in better balance. Daily my spirit shouts for me to practice moderation yet I seldom listen. But . . . I am still sincerely trying.

## 6. <u>BE HONEST</u>

This was truly Manuel's great strength. I do not recall Manuel ever lying to me or anyone. I do not remember him exaggerating or embellishing. I do not believe I ever heard him belittle anyone, intentionally harm or hurt them, or say or do something solely for his own gain. I mean this, and I know it to be quite rare.

Manuel meant what he said, and said what he meant. This led him to live a life of substantial integrity, dignity, and maturity.

I, on the other hand, was consumed with being popular, and this led me to often talk a good line, say what someone needed to hear, or to work hard at putting myself in the best light. My need to keep everyone happy, be "the good boy," also led me to hover near the truth, but often not land there.

Both of us felt strongly about this basic aspect of character. In today's world, with so much lying and deceit and "bull", the value of honesty cannot be stressed enough. Paying attention to being honest, is a discipline well worth mastering. It is the heart of leading a genuinely good life.

> *Manuel meant what he said, and said what he meant.*
> *This led him to live a life of substantial*
> *integrity, dignity, and maturity.*

## 7. BE REAL

Manuel had amazing radar for phoniness. I doubt anyone ever thought of Manuel as being artificial, fake, or a manipulator. His integrity was superb. It seemed to be innate. I don't think he had to think about being real, he just was. It had become his second nature. He was quite congruent as a soul.

I have to work at being real. I am a performer. I can be a chameleon. I do have to remember and expect myself to be true to who I really am. For me, being real was more a choice and a daily decision.

Both of us felt that being real was critical to a good and hopeful life. We saw it as essential. Living in America, where even our reality shows are fake, it is wise to work hard at being authentic, genuine, and the real deal.

If we ask ourselves, whom do we trust, we will likely find it is those individuals we experience as being substantial and true.

## 8. GETTING DOWN TO GROWING UP

Here we came to a very substantial and mutual conclusion. This became a consistent topic of our discussions. It was, for us, the spiritual issue which dwarfed all others.

Our culture is grossly immature—too concerned about accumulating stuff we do not even need, or at times, want. We often behave like spoiled brats. Arrogant. Self-centered. Selfish. Lacking in compassion, courage, and creativity. We refuse to address problems, conflicts, and chaos in our personal lives. In addition, we can be unresponsive to obvious social needs crying out for our involvement and investment.

If we get down to growing up, and choose to mature as a society, we can then admit and address how we are running out of time in applying our energy, ingenuity, and resources, to the glaring issues of climate change, racism, violence, greed, and an immense gap between the rich and the poor.

If there is one place where our lack of maturity shows most clearly, it is in our lack of initiative to create a livable future for our children. Our youth are frequently bemoaning our lack of adult presence and leadership. We adults have too often given our children everything imaginable, but failed to offer them the vital and gracious gift of real hope.

Hope in the future is now fully in the hands of those mature enough to make it happen, to make the choices, decisions, and sacrifices necessary. Those who are willing to be strong and fiercely courageous in their determination can build a saner and safer world for all.

## 9. HAVE A STRONG WORK ETHIC

I have long felt that Manuel, at heart, was basically a pretty old-fashioned guy. A true gentleman, he showed respect for his elders. He was polite, modest, and kind. He was that guy who would give the shirt off his back, open the door, and make life easier for those he loved.

Manuel also had a strong old-fashioned work ethic. He believed deeply in being reliable and responsible. He was big on follow through and staying true to his word. He took great pride in feeling he had done his best.

I remember when Coach Fishbain, our legendary football coach at Horlick High School, told Manuel he was to be our starting center.

I am telling you the truth, nobody worked harder than Manuel to be the very best, and when he was named to the All-City team, every single player among us knew just how much he deserved the honor.

Manuel felt his family had taught him the value of hard work. He often spoke of his parents being great role models when it came to putting in a full day's effort to provide for the family. Both of his parents, like mine, and so many others, worked tirelessly and without complaint, to make good homes for us.

Manuel had a briefcase. He was given it when he was accepted into an accelerated program at Washington Junior High School. Manuel talked about the importance of that briefcase, which I believe he kept until he passed, and how it represented to him the reality that his education was his job—he graduated second in our high school class of nearly 1000.

His academic achievements speak for themselves. A Ph.D. from the University of Oregon, and a full professorship at Arizona State University, are the result of a diligent and determined desire to learn.

I loved calling him Professor Barrera. He loved calling me The Very Wrong Reverend.

I told him I never saw him hand in a late assignment or take a test unprepared. The guy made it difficult for the rest of us to compete—and I competed with Manuel in everything.

I must admit to arguing with Manuel about keeping this on the list of what mattered most. I cautioned about our American tendency to create a bevy of workaholics and how we failed to encourage rest and relaxation and re-creation. Manuel held firm.

I didn't surrender here. I simply came to agree with my friend's assessment.

Our culture does need to take greater pride in the quality and even the quantity of our work. We cannot be a nation which knows the price of everything, but the value of nothing. We must take pride in our work; not a greedy demanding pride, but a belief in caring about what we create.

His work ethic is probably the reason why I never considered not completing this manuscript.

## 10. ENJOY

Manuel asked me at one point, "What was the best advice you have for the parent of a teenager or young adult?"

I told him the truth, and it was very simple, "Just enjoy them!"

We are so damn busy all the time, so stressed, tired, burned out and up and down, we often do not have the energy to be present for our lives, or theirs, let alone to actually enjoy our children.

Joy is a jump, a leap up to higher ground. It is a perspective and attitude and choice. It is knowing how and when to receive. Joy is being conscious of savoring the sweetness of each day, and claiming as many chances as we can, to enjoy those we love a great deal.

Happiness just comes when it wishes. It is a bit flighty and noncommittal. Happiness is like the butterfly which occasionally perches on our shoulder. It is there, and then it is gone.

Joy is deeper, fuller, and committed. It is a knowing, a trust, a belief, and a decision. It is the counting of blessings. It is having our priorities in order. It is being satisfied. It is looking at a teenager, or young adult, and seeing them through God's eyes, and then feeling a swarming Grace which informs us they are beloved, and we as parents, are being good enough.

Then we try a little bit harder.

(By the way, I have never heard a father speak of a daughter with greater devotion and pride, than Manuel about Lea. He truly did enjoy her completely. She was literally his pride and his joy. She was, in many respects, his very best friend, and I suspect, vice versa.)

## 11. **DARE TO DREAM**

Manuel and I both tended to play it safe. We both needed and valued security. We came from homes which would now be classified as "pretty poor," or as Manuel would say, "There was nothing all that pretty about it."

We both were ambitious and worked hard. We had high expectations. However, taking a risk, or dreaming big, was just not in our genes.

We kept our dreams quiet and our hopes secret. We made sure we had popular approval of any plans we named or claimed.

We both wished we had taken a few more risks, wished we'd worried less about failing or disappointing or being thought the fool. We both knew we may never have become some great visionary, but we wished we had tried to "fly" now and then. We would have been pleased, as the saying goes, to have shot for the moon, because even if we had missed, we would have landed among the stars.

We both considered one another a star. Not a celebrity, but a shining light for others. We were big fans of each other.

Still, we wished we had not been so timid. We wondered what might have been had we truly followed our bliss or our longings. We were both satisfied...BUT...

## 12. **FIGHT HARDER FOR WHAT YOU BELIEVE IN**

This came as a complete surprise to me. Manuel was extremely frustrated, disappointed, and angry with himself, for not having fought harder for the racial respect and equality he wanted for the entire Hispanic Community.

Manuel told me numerous tales of being belittled or treated in a bigoted manner. He had a horrible experience when, as a child, he went to see his father's family in Texas. He was denied access to restaurants and stores for the first time, and was always the one selected to buy his baby brother his milk—he had the lightest skin.

I remember an incident at Washington Junior High, when I got my first taste of the bigotry he faced. He and I were talking before a Student Council Meeting, and a few of the ninth grade girls, also on the Council, were talking about a party that weekend. One of the girls said, "I am not sure if my folks will let me go . . . there might be Mexicans there."

When I shared that story with Manuel, he remembered it clearly. In fact, he said, every such comment of a racist nature, is indelibly imprinted on his memory and heart. He also told me that I started to talk so loudly, to cover up the ninth grade girl chatter, he had to tell me to stop yelling.

Even in the conducting of his Ph.D. oral exams, Manuel knew his race was a major factor in the questions asked and comments made. He told me to **not** share the specifics. Our conversations did get quite political. We did not, however, wish to use this book as a platform for our views. We did feel, however, it was necessary to acknowledge when our politics were clearly informing and shaping our values, morals, and ethics.

We were both deeply disturbed by the surge in White Supremacy thinking and behavior in America. We found former President Trump to be a catalyst for the arrival of blatantly racist and even fascist politics, as evidenced by the January insurrection at the Capital—this was demonstrably a white riot or coup.

I would hope our readers would be aware of why this could not be left out, and still be true to Manuel's vision and voice for a better America, and better Americans. The intent has not been to offend. The desire is to be honest about our shared core beliefs for our nation.

I intend to continue to fight hard in calling adolescents to a genuine maturity. I hope for them to become adults who know how to serve, sacrifice, and even suffer on behalf of their ethical convictions.

I will also encourage them to celebrate equality and diversity, be compassionate, respectful, kind, merciful and gracious . . . all of which are the attributes of true maturity.

I will keep on fighting for the idea we can come together and save this planet, restore a sense of racial and religious respect for all, and to strive for a simpler, saner, gentler, and smarter way of living.

Manuel wanted to finish this chapter with an open letter to our readers, in which we would speak to how we might have done it differently, if we had had the chance. Though this was Manuel's intention, with both of us still having some time to actually make needed changes, or to live a slightly transformed life, this was just not to be.

Still, I will try, once again, to capture the tone and texture of many of our conversations on the theme—"If I could do it over!"

*Dear Reader,*

*If we could have done it over, we would have had more fun. We would have chased beauty around more. We would have worked harder on the stuff which matters and which lasts eternally. We would have worried less about the opinion of others, and more about being in tune with our Higher Power—as we understand that concept.*

*We would have shown more interest, compassion, respect, mercy and love, and would have communicated it on a far more regular basis. We would have spoken up and out on our deepest core convictions.*

*We would have tried hard to avoid being burned out, exhausted, or highly stressed, because it does not encourage creativity or compassion, and definitely inhibits love—it crushes forgiveness.*

*We would have wrestled with our questions and doubts, as well as our hopes and dreams, and sought to find a community of friends to serve as a context to mature, grow, and learn to the very end. We would have invested more time and energy in our true friendships.*

*We would have sought out community. We would have looked for a community which enabled us to embrace the wilderness, the darkness, the mystery, the longings, the yearnings, and our deepest desires. We would have sought out a context which was truly creative and committed.*

*We would have worked to have a positive attitude, a productive perspective, and to be a spiritual presence of love, life, laughter, and lifelong learning. We would have let ourselves get silly, even play the fool, and step wildly outside of the box now and then.*

*We would have done nothing more often. We would have said nothing more often, especially when we had nothing of real value to say. We would have listened more, looked deeper, and savored the wondrous bittersweet moments which make life rich.*

*We would have made more of an effort to live and die well. We would have celebrated being human. We would have known we were enough. We were beloved. We were meant to behold this earth of ours and honor our chance to be alive. We would have become global citizens.*

*We would have been pleased and satisfied, even celebrated, how much our friends and family knew they were loved by us, and though we could have done better, we gave it a hell of an effort.*

*Our wives and our children knew how much they mattered, and how unforgettable they were—we fully trusted that, and this was an incessant source of our happiness and joy. The way I will live in the time I have left, will strive to honor the immense impact of this once in a lifetime friendship. Good friendships matter, because they collect the good stories, encourage the good deeds, and enable us to be good people with good hearts. The real good life. The good life to which America must return.*

*Manuel made such a difference in my life, and in so many others. He made our lives better. He improved the condition of the planet and the people on it.*

*Think about it. He was never mean. He was never greedy. He was never manipulative. He was never less than his best. I never heard him lie or even dent the Truth. He was always hoping to do and be more. He never quit, and after 40 years with MS, he had good reason to wonder about waving the white flag. He never did. I thank God for that!*

*Remember, there are no do overs. There can, however, be a chance for days spent in focus, centered, grounded, and rooted deeply in Grace. Do not fritter away your blessed days. Seize the day. Receive it. Be glad in it. Say thanks for the gift.*

*Most sincerely . . .*
*on behalf of Manuel Barrera*
*and Bill Grimbol*

"To be without love is to be without grace, which is what matters most in life. We is so much better than I."
—James Patterson

# Lesson Two:

# DO NOT SQUANDER YOUR FORTUNE

> Busy with the ugliness of expensive success
> We forget the easiness of free beauty
> Lying sad right around the corner,
> Only an instant removed,
> Unnoticed and squandered.
> –Dejan Stojanovic

"Measure wealth not by the things you have, but by the things you have for which you would not take money."
–Anonymous

This chapter is devoted to a decidedly religious theme. The key word here is fortune. What do we value most? What do we consider precious? What do we cherish? What gives our lives their point and purpose, meaning, and worth? What is it that we could not possibly live without?

This question of fortune is a major aspect of almost every religion on the planet, and even for those who consider themselves to be atheist, agnostic, or simply and solely spiritual. Our fortune shapes and defines our value system, and thereby, it critically influences how we spend our days.

At one point in our lives, both Manuel and I were quite religious. We were members of Christian churches, and found in Jesus, a guide and the event of Grace itself. We strove to obey the doctrines and dogmas of our denominations, in my case, Lutheran and then Presbyterian, and for Manuel, a more fundamentalist denomination, The Church of Christ.

I was ordained clergy. In the process of writing this book, I came to find out that Manuel was also very much a minister in his own right. He preached. He taught. He studied Scripture. At UW-Eau Claire, his dorm mates called him "the minister." I suspect this meant Manuel rigorously followed his religion and adhered to its values, which included no drinking or dancing, and made it clear sex was out of bounds—something either sacred or dirty, with nothing in between.

Manuel and I argued often about religion. Manuel sought to save my soul, and believed the goal of life was getting into heaven. I felt that life's big goal was to build God's Kingdom here on earth. I saw heaven as something out of my control, and therefore, of little worry or interest. I felt it vital to help the poor, bind the brokenhearted, and lift up the downtrodden. Manuel believed in all of this as well, but being saved was paramount to his religion.

I got angry with him about not dancing. I was furious he would not attend the numerous parties being held in the backyards and basements of classmates, and how he oddly expressed no interest in making-out with the harem of girls who were attracted to him.

However, one Friday night he did come to a gathering at Dave Zelinski's house, and when I came downstairs with a Pepsi for him, anxious for him to enjoy himself, found him making out with Marita Simic, who was happily draped across his lap. I knew then, there were some cracks in this religious wall, and became determined to knock that sucker down.

Ironically, both of us moved away from the Church, and from the dogmas and doctrines and creeds we found confining, conforming, and more importantly, of little to no interest, or application to our lives. I have become pretty much a Unitarian in spirit, and Manuel claims what I would feel comfortable calling, a somewhat powerful Higher Power.

We both still respect the Church and the seeking which can spawn religion. We simply had grown out of being treated like children, and sought a faith and spirituality which was profoundly mature. We had no interest in being a religious clone.

We questioned everything. We doubted often. We didn't feel locked into a certain set of beliefs. We didn't claim to have all the answers, or even some of them. We just acknowledged a spiritual life, which we experienced with all our senses, and on most days in our lives.

We believed in serving others, sacrificing on behalf of the whole, and suffering with and for humanity. We both felt there was nothing more important than trying to improve the lives of others, and to relieve the anxiety, fear, worry, poverty, or oppression, in which they may live.

Though we moved a great distance from our religious training and upbringing, and I from the vows I took to be ordained, we still found the topic to be tender and tempting; even tantalizing. Our conversations were intense and deep, filled with respect for hearing the other's viewpoint. Oh my—maturity can make so many things more enjoyable and productive.

Let me turn to explaining why we both felt it so important to not squander our fortune. First, let me state clearly what we felt our own treasures to be. Second, let me speak to how we may choose to squander our fortune—and why. Thirdly, and finally, let me offer insight into the spiritual impact of squandering, as individuals, couples, families, communities, nations, and our world.

## OUR FORTUNES

Here we were clones of one another. Very little difference at all. Our fortune was our chance to be alive, and to love, and to learn. We mutually spoke of the gift of our marriages and our children. They were our lived blessing, and the reason for getting up in the morning, a great source of our worry, wonder, and hope.

Love is our fortune. We both loved to read, write, and think. We loved to teach and preach. We loved seeking and finding great friends. We wished we had done even more for our families. We hoped our nation might get back to goodness, rather than some silly and dangerous obsession with greatness—which appears to be a very selective and very white attainment.

Our health is our fortune and no one knew this better than Manuel. He accepted his disease, but rabidly sought to find as many healthy moments, attitudes, and experiences as he could.

Kindness, compassion, care, concern, patience, perseverance, and the willingness to put others before ourselves, were all component parts of our concept of fortune. A fortune is what we must share with others. Our fortune is our earth, and everyone who inhabits the planet. Our fortune is for all time—eternal. The love of neighbor as self is at the core of most religions and remains the primary cause and catalyst for most spiritual growth and maturation.

Our sense of the Divine is our fortune. We each get hints and hunches as to what is our Higher Power, and why it is crucial to follow in its footsteps or path. We are wealthy and wise when we come to know and understand that the ways of the world are seldom the ways of a God or Higher Power. It is fortunate when we take the road less traveled, and risk becoming the person we were created to be.

The NOW is our greatest fortune. It was our first fortune, and it will be our last—at least during our lifetimes.

We were never meant to live in the past, only to learn from it. There is no way we can actually retreat into what were often called "the good old days." Those days are indeed officially gone. They are not forgotten, however, and we can visit our memories any time we wish. Still, if we become obsessed with our memories, we fail to live in the present, and this is a true squandering of fortune.

Living in the past is something we often speak of casually, but I caution all of us on how compulsive this can become. It may start off innocently enough, as recalling days we loved in the past, or which are remembered with an almost idyllic reverence. If this becomes a habit, and then an oft-repeated pattern, it can easily erode our present, consuming each day with the notion the present can never measure up.

This is dangerous, and as a pastor, I witnessed many older folks, like myself, spend so much time reviewing the past, they have little time or effort or energy to invest in the day at hand.

I love my memories . . . at the end, for Manuel, his memories gave him great comfort . . . we both could have been called nostalgia freaks. However, we knew ourselves well enough to know we would work hard at taming our memories. We wanted to enjoy them, not obsess over them; plus, we wished to give the NOW a fair chance—and the NOW can never compete with a past we have declared perfect.

My grandmother, Othilia, once told me the good old days were better because the people were better. She may have had a valid point there, however, when she got so livid with her neighbor Anne, she would not even say hello to her, I reminded her how she had taught me to love my neighbor as myself. She told me I had made a good point, and brought a fresh loaf of bread and an apology to Anne that very afternoon.

This kept her from squandering a lifelong friendship, which eventually brought her untold comfort and care.

We are also not meant to live in the future. We are encouraged to not worry, fret, or feel anxious, about a time over which we have little to no control. All we have is the present. The NOW is the fortune, and no matter how much time we spend speculating on the fortunes which may come, we cannot offer this imagined future any certainty, or guarantee, let alone a warranty.

Tomorrow will be what it will be. It will have its fair share of joy, happiness, sorrow, and tragedy. We cannot truly predict, other than an educated guess, where the future will wander.

Manuel and I were both dreamers and daydreamers, but I scored more points on the daydreaming scale. Manuel was far more practical. The fact remains, we both loved to do either one. We both considered ourselves advocates for everyone to do a good deal of both. Still, there would come a time when we knew we must cease the fantasizing. This was only because, once again, dreaming and daydreaming can so easily become an avoidance of coping creatively with the here and now.

Our allegiance was to the present. If we paid attention to the creation, addressing its protection and maintenance, we would have done our best to protect the reality of the future. We cannot dictate or determine the flow of the future. We can, however, live in the present in such a way, we do not manage to dam it up or divert it.

I explained to Manuel that one of the aspects of his earlier religion which I truly despised, was its emphasis on the afterlife. I did not believe we had any idea where or what heaven would be like, let alone who would be there—if it is even a "there." I told him I believed we had the here and now, and we could build or create heaven today . . . the NOW was fit for our use, and only the NOW. I also made it clear I had only found a glimpse or glance of heaven in this very same here and now.

He told me he wished he had believed the same much earlier in his life, as he spent way too much time during his adolescence and early adulthood, fretting on whether he would earn enough points to get through the pearly gates. He also said he had come to think of God, or a Higher Power, or Spirit, as being far gentler and most gracious, one who did not keep track of flaws or mistakes.

He also made it quite clear, he no longer thought much about heaven as a time or place, but for him, it had become the hope of being whole again. I told him I thought of heaven as actually melting into my Higher Power, becoming one with, or joining forces. Manuel spoke of it as being able to walk, run, swim, and bike.

Both lovely and wondrous images!

Do we think of each day as a fortune? It is a powerful and profound perspective. It will serve to remind us to seize the day, receive its lessons and gifts, explore its questions and doubts, and examine all the possibilities presented to us. If we see the NOW as our fortune, we will be more prone to be productive, positive, and purposefully creative.

I know, when many of us hear the phrase, "live in the moment" or "be in the now", we shrug our shoulders, roll our eyes, and wonder what this really means. Being a cynic comes easily to all of us at times, and it manages to pry open the need to question the value of anything and everything; except what we can make money doing, or spend money being.

There is no fortune to be found in putting the nose to grindstone, just a bloody nose. Finding the pot of gold at the end of the rainbow, while missing the rainbow, is to squander the fortune as a whole. It remains true—we cannot take it with us, and there are no pockets in a shroud. It is simply a very difficult lesson to embrace as Truth.

The chance to have a good or beautiful or meaningful or lovely day, is no small achievement. It requires the soul to be present, a heart to risk being bloodied or broken, and the consideration of every possible failure or flaw which might occur. Under such perilous circumstances, to still take the chance of making someone's day, or filling our own to the very brim, is an act of courage, conviction, and character.

Every single day contains myriad fortunes and most are readily available to those who seek to find them.

## OUR SQUANDERING

When we squander, we are wasting something or someone of immense value. We are choosing to ignore the vital importance or purpose of what and whom we love. We are being detached and apathetic to that which matters most. We are pursuing what will not last, is possibly artificial or phony, and can cause the soul to become cold, callous, and even conniving.

We squander our fortune whenever we are being arrogant or superior. Thinking we are better than someone, feeling that someone is of less value than ourselves or those we choose to love, is an offense to our God or our Higher Power. Elitism of any kind is so fringed in indifference and apathy, so prone to hatred and judgment, it withers our capacity to love.

When we stop loving, we are squandering our fortune to the max.

We squander our fortune when we are being selfish or greedy. Manuel and I both believed our American culture was falling victim to a selfishness and greed, which had significantly lowered our moral leadership around the world. How the world witnessed America as a people, a nation, and as a culture, was still something our generation believed was of importance. We agreed. We wanted America to be worthy of respect and honor again.

Selfishness and greed are emblematic of a soul in decline. They are evidence of a lack of pursuing goodness in our lifestyle or morality. As a nation, we have a spirit which is easily enflamed and enraged, often looking for a war to start, or an enemy or scapegoat to blame.

In our last conversation on this specific theme, the impact of greed and selfishness, Manuel and I agreed wholeheartedly. These two characteristics, we adamantly believed, must not be parts of our legacies. To be called greedy or selfish, would have disappointed either of us to the very core of our being.

We squander our fortune when we try to be perfect, please everyone, or live a life of pretense and pretend. Perfectionism is always demoralizing, and thus, it will ultimately bring out the very worst in us.

People pleasing keeps our relationships shamefully shallow, lacking in depth, integrity, and maturity. People pleasing encourages "fair weather" friends, those who are around only when convenient or there is something in it for them—some material benefit to be had. In these chaotic and frenzied times, we all need friends who will be there when the going gets tough or when we are running on empty.

People who play pretend in life are void of maturity, lacking in soul, and may have become worthless fakes. These are folks who are in it for the show, the image, the stuff, and the chance to get rich quick. They are frequently liars, con artists, and on the prowl for the quick fix or money-making scam.

We squander our fortune when we choose to be lazy. Laziness is (shows?) a lack of character. It often reveals the absence of a spine or a soul. Beings of little depth, few convictions, and no real strength of character—spiritually, they have grown flabby. Laziness is not about the need of rest, but choosing to rest while watching others do the work, and then complaining about how the work was done.

Laziness is not attractive, productive, or worthy of respect. Lazy folks often talk a good line, claim great talents and gifts, but have no real factual evidence to show for it—it is a fact only in their head, which is already badly bloated.

We squander our fortune when we are addicted or compulsive. An addiction is a belief that we cannot live without something or someone. This belief leads to compulsive and often dangerous, even lethal behavior, and to becoming a full-blown absence of a presence.

Of the two of us, I was the expert on addiction. I cannot name an addiction for which I fail to qualify; other than Paranoid's Anonymous, because nobody will tell me where those meetings are held. This is what I know of addiction—it will eventually demand everything,

everything you claim to cherish and adore in life. When you have lost control, your life grown unmanageable, then you will tragically and compulsively squander your fortune as well.

It is exactly like falling dominos.

The end of every addiction is either a bottom or a grave. The damage and loss involved is significant, substantial, and savage. It will ultimately strip you of everything and everyone you hold dear.

If you can read the story of Betty Ford's intervention, when her family and select friends confronted her lovingly, about how painful it was to watch her alcoholism squander her fortune and how much suffering they had each endured as a result. Squandering is often most punishing of those we claim to dearly love.

The only way the addict can survive creating so much pain is to live in denial, lie compulsively, or find a good scapegoat to blame. Remember, we may survive a bit longer by denial, but others are often maimed and harmed and scarred permanently in the process.

We squander our fortune when we waste time. Think about it. Wasting time—what a dishonor to our God or Higher Power. What a lack of gratitude. What a failure to count blessings. How painful it is to watch someone fritter away their talents or skills by simply failing to practice or discipline them. How ridiculous to be gifted, and throw it out with the garbage, without ever opening the package, reading the directions, making an effort, actually trying, or taking the risk.

Gifts are given. We all have them. Yes, each and every one of us. We know our gifts, by noticing what it is we are doing or being, when we lose track of time. When we have lost track of time, we have entered heaven, which is the absence of time, and there we can lay claim to what comes naturally to us, second nature, and we know to be divinely given or sanctioned.

We squander our fortune when we fritter things away, or just keep on dabbling, never making a concerted and committed effort to actualize our dreams. Frittering away a gift, or dabbling with our talents, is not simply a waste, it is a choice to squander, to knowingly refuse to put in the time or effort or work required.

Every single morning of much of my childhood, my grandmother, Othilia Hjortness, baked eight loaves of homemade bread. One was for her, and the rest were distributed to her children, who all lived in Racine, Wisconsin, at that time. I once asked her why she did that, especially considering she got up at 4 a.m. each morning to do so.

"Well, I make amazing bread Billy, everyone says so, and to be honest, I work out all my problems while I am doing it. (She always whistled why she ironed or baked.) So, I came to the conclusion this was something I not only loved to do, but was meant to do. Plus, it was the last remaining way to know my children still needed me—of course, lavished with butter, but still . . .

"I think my bread makes God happy Billy. I just know that for a fact. My heart tells me it is true."

I never told her how much I agreed with her, but I had, and still do.

## TAKING PERSONAL INVENTORY

As you can tell, one of the chief ways Manuel and I created the lengthy outline for this manuscript, was by compiling lists, and ranking and reminding ourselves which we believed were of greatest importance. We found the lists helpful and focusing. After Manuel died, I found our lists to be powerful visual reminders of the themes we hoped to cover and share with our readers.

At this point, I want to share my perspective, my personal inventory, of how we each did in being true, congruent to our stated priorities, goals, dreams—OUR FORTUNE.

When Manuel spoke of his wife Aurelia and his daughter Lea, his voice would change. It became slower, lower, steeped in such love and trust and respect. They were the pinnacle of his treasure.

There was one call Manuel got from Lea, when she was quite upset at being mistreated by a superior at her company. It was obvious. If Manuel could have called this "superior inferior," he would have ripped him up one side and down the other. Then Manuel calmed, and stated he knew Lea would soon get past the wrong suffered, and would take care of it.

I told him how I loved seeing him so filled with devotion for his daughter. He told me she was his world.

At the very end, from all I have gathered by phone conversations, Aurelia significantly helped to gently toss Manuel to the other side, just as she had enabled him, on so many days, to enjoy his life. I think of it like swinging a child back and forth, while they kick and scream, but then are delighted to be released, feel the glorious water, and make a huge splash. They run back, to do it all again.

I think Manuel's treasure was also teaching. He wanted to be a truly good teacher. This meant competence and caring to him. He cared so deeply about his students and he worked hard to make sure they were truly learning.

I always found Manuel to be brilliant. I mean that. It simply shimmered and shown. Manuel's life was a lesson being offered. He lived in such a way, we could pause and consider every word he said, simply because the source from which it came was so damn pure and impeccable, so thickly coated in love.

His family was also his treasure. He cherished them. He adored them. He respected each of them, as individuals, as parents and siblings.

He told me how his father was charming, charismatic, witty, wise, and wonderful when he was within the Hispanic community—he was a significant leader in League of United Latin American Citizens in Racine. He also sadly explained how his father disappeared around white folks. He spoke meekly, being very shy, and with a noticeable loss of power and self-respect—this bothered Manuel tremendously.

Manuel did ponder his father's fractured life and often considered its impact on his own. He found it to be a puzzle with a missing piece; he never got close enough to his dad to ask the reason why; it never seemed the right time, or, there was simply not enough time.

Manuel's mother is a force. I personally still get a real kick out of her. She is spunky and witty and wise and can be a real whirling dervish—though health issues are slowing her down a bit, as they do us all as we age.

When I had lunch with her at Park INN, a favorite haunt of Manuel's and mine, she spoke with such adoring words and tones, and I loved hearing her be 100% mother. Manuel had recently gotten her a new car, and she was just so pleased and proud. I told Manuel, and of course, he had a hard time hearing he had touched her deeply—he was sooooo modest. I, on the other hand, would have taken out ads with photos of me presenting the car to my mother; but thank God, Hedwig never got her license.

Manuel's sister, Linda, was definitely Manuel's confidante, and he believed he could and would tell her anything and everything. His respect for her was immense. His trust in her, full. She was a very calming presence for him.

Manuel's love for Liz was just as deep, but it was aimed at enabling Liz to enjoy and be content with her own gifts, talents, and abilities. He did recognize what a powerfully spiritual person she was, and what a deep soul she had.

When I was in high school with him, I thought of Manuel's brother David as his appendage. David loved being with Manuel. Manuel so enjoyed having David with him. Manuel regretted being too hard on David, expecting too much, and felt he was often way too parental. He told me on several occasions, he just wished he had simply enjoyed and affirmed David more.

I told Manuel what I believed—that he **was** parental with David. I also told him that I always felt he was doing so, not only out of love, but in an effort to enable David to become all he could be.

If David ever wonders if he had earned his brother's love and respect, the answer is a resounding YES. However, his expectations of David were extraordinarily high. I think this is probably true of most fathers and big brothers.

Gary was the brother Manuel felt he never got to know well. It felt like the physical distance between them impacted their relationship, as did the progression of Manuel's illness. I am not sure if Manuel had the energy or spirit to be fully present in Gary's life. When Manuel spoke of Gary, he always made it clear he knew his brother was a really good man, had a good soul, and he was proud of him.

With Gary, I think Manuel felt a bit cheated. MS took away the gift of mobility, and getting to be a real presence. This was a sadness for Manuel, but not a regret.

To the whole Barrera crew, of which I feel I am an honorary member: I want you to know you were treasured by Manuel—you were and are and always will be, a major piece of his fortune.

As for myself, my fortune was also my family. Boy, do we need to be reminded of that on a regular basis. How easily and quickly we can wander away from what gives us our deepest and fullest satisfaction. Both Manuel and I deeply regretted the enormous amount of time and energy we wasted on people-pleasing and performing, trying to be the best, trying to curb our critics, trying to make a mark in Life's hide. Those actions wasted precious time we could have spent with family.

We both simply wished we had had more fun, enjoyed our families more, and celebrated the gift of each day and this blessed beautiful earth. Trying to be successful in a career, or to make a big difference, is not all a waste of time. There is much good to be said of it, but on the whole, we are never as busy or as important or indispensable as we think.

John Lennon was right when he said, "Life is what happens to you while you're busy making other plans."

Christine was the great love of my life, and a woman of fierce convictions and power, a wildly talented minister with a superb speaking and singing voice. Her insight and sensitivity to the needs of others were remarkable. Christine's mercy was epic, and her graciousness in crisis unparalleled.

We both battled the addiction of compulsive overeating, and it cost us dearly. In the end, Christine died from complications following her second gastric bypass surgery—she was just 55.

She had arrived on Long Island at 165 pounds, and died in 2020, fifteen years later, at 415. In the eighteen months after her death, I put on 120 pounds, and have never been able to get it all off. I think, on some crazy level of my being, my weight keeps all the issues of our marriage, and Christine, alive.

She was an extraordinary and funny and fun mother to her great joy, our son, Justin. When he asked her at age six, if sex was as messy as it sounded, she calmly responded, "Only if it is done right." She took him out of school once a month, for an adventure day, taught him to ride the subway in NYC, see Broadway shows, ski and skate and sled, and to ride a horse on the ocean beach, and even navigate the rapids on a raft.

Patty was one of Christine's best friends, and we married two years after Chris died. Patty was a lot like Aunt Bea of Mayberry fame, and she was indeed the perfect pastor's wife. We entertained a lot, held spiritual and biblical classes in our home, and took small groups on retreat. She was quite simply, the kindest woman I ever knew.

We formed a group called Young at Heart, with whom we went all over New England, eating and shopping and having fun, soaking in the raw beauty of the seasons. Our Christmas Shoppe barn tour was a personal favorite of mine; but most of all, I enjoyed playing Ralph Cramden, and driving our 15-seat van; my, oh my, could we sing and joke and create some heavy-duty mirth.

Patty loved to bake, cook, clean, entertain, sing, dance, and was the director of the Senior Citizen program on Shelter Island. Caring was her calling, and she was superb at it. She lifted spirits, enabled hope, and comforted one and all.

Justin is my biggest critic and fan. His words matter to me, as they are spot on. He knows me. He also expects the best from me. He challenges me to change. He confronts me when I am being manipulative or phony. He reprimands me when I am whining for no good reason. In his own quite practical way, Justin's love for me is deeply spiritual, and rooted in a belief that I can make an amazing difference for others, when I am in focus and in balance.

Jay is my chosen son, and has been a part of the family since he was sixteen. He is a wonderful artist, has an agile and gifted mind, and is one of the funniest characters I know—especially in consort with Justin. He has brought so much to my life, and I cherish his presence more and more every day. He is an original. One of a kind. He has his own unique signature style. Think macabre Renaissance.

I believe Manuel and I savored our fortune, but unfortunately, also squandered a good bit of it. We had good families, the blessing of children, and a few strong friends. However, we were also too consumed with our image, and definitely worked overtime to prove our worth and value, dependability, and to be—well, the good guys. We were high achievers, and regularly did more than we were asked. Our schedules were kept loaded, and if the truth be known, we both felt we were never enough.

I think I can speak for Manuel here. Not squandering our fortune is primarily an issue of maintaining balance. We both knew when we were being lopsided in our lifestyles, but found ourselves to be quite compulsive in our habits. We failed to rest or play or have fun, as much as we should have or could have. It was a deep regret. We experienced a feeling of swarming sadness, and a loss of something quite precious.

I am still not sure why, so many of the men of my generation, had such a compulsive need to prove themselves, and were so highly prone to becoming workaholics. By the time we got around to taking a break, we were often too tired to enjoy it.

Another sad truth was how we often spent our recreation time with the guys, playing the same sports we did as adolescents, maybe with the addition of golf, tennis, jogging, hiking, biking, or swimming. Nothing wrong with this, except we never seemed to learn how to be quiet, still, reflective, or just enjoy being with our family.

Both of us felt we had neglected the more spiritual aspects of our lives, and found ourselves pushing too hard and sailing too seldom. Sailing is nothing more than setting our sails to capture the wind. We tried to be both the sail and the wind. It was exhausting, and without knowing it, we were frequently burned out. This often led to our families getting the leftovers, or being placed on the back burner.

Our true fortune is not meant to be saved or even spent. It is to be savored and enjoyed. This was something our generation simply did not advocate or even practice. Our generation was a champion of hard work, being industrious, and to be honest, bragged about not needing much rest. The result was that our health, families, and lives paid a price. We did not necessarily ignore our spiritual state or status, but we did not make it a priority.

Manuel and I talked extensively about how we felt guilty when just having fun, or ashamed of doing nothing. We thought of being busy as what mattered, declaring our purpose and value. We both thought it was rather sad, how in America many families plan all year long for a two- week vacation—after working full bore for fifty.

Think of it this way. When we are coming to the close of our work life, or even our days on this earth, we do not yearn for more work to do. Our longings are seldom about wanting to buy something else. As we age, we gain focus, and what we desire most are those wondrous transforming moments of joy. This means family and friends and the steadfast beauty of the earth.

We both wanted our readers to understand how we did gain real satisfaction from our careers, but it was with family, while playing, re-creating, exploring or examining something brand new, or doing some ritual we always enjoyed immensely, where we found our joy and balance.

Most of us work hard. Too hard. We get burned out. The obligations and duties keep rising, and the rewards and gratifications keep declining. The fire in the hearth goes out, and when it does, it will take considerable time and effort to rebuild.

Work on being in good balance. Take sabbath days. Think of them as holy days. Make holidays a part of the plan as often as we can. This will strengthen our soul, and give fullness to our days. This is a piece of advice we both wished we had followed more rigorously.

> "A holiday gives one a chance to look backward and
> forward, to reset oneself by an inner compass."
> –May Sarton, *At Seventy: A Journal*

# Lesson Three:

# COMING BACK TO LIFE, ON LIFE'S TERMS

"One of the most powerful things I'd learned since getting sober is to love and accept life on life's terms. Alcoholics have a hard time doing this; we're little id-driven crybabies, guzzling and complaining about how nothing in this life goes the way we think it should. Accepting and even embracing the world as it is can be radical, and it can have powerful, positive results."
–Michelle Tea

"Acceptance doesn't mean life gets better; it just means that my way of living on life's terms improves."
–Sharon E. Rainey

Manuel and I both acknowledged that at some point, for some reason, without knowing why, we had gotten somewhat off track. We remained active, productive, and busy trying to be good at what we did for a living, as well as meeting the expectations of our families, friends, and our omnipresent culture. Still, we both spoke of knowing something was off, adrift, and that we felt anxious, alienated, and at times, alone.

I don't believe this was ever an event in either of our lives, and I am not referring to something wicked, or vile, or an addiction—though we both were compulsive about keeping everyone happy, and performing at top speed much of the time. Manuel fought hard to not let MS slow him down, or to keep others and himself, from noticing if it had.

No, I'm referring to something far more subtle, swarming, and spiritual—something about the state of our soul. We did not speak of it and certainly did not claim it as an issue. It was just there. We both knew it. We sensed it, felt its presence, and were puzzled by it. Recently, we just blamed it on aging, and to some extent, blame could be placed there.

In retrospect, we both came to the same conclusion. Though our lives were relatively positive, definitely productive, even successful in many respects, we knew something was missing. I mentioned to Manuel how I was a great list maker, but how it had dawned on me that I was seldom on the list, and neither was my Higher Power. I was trying to be perfect, but trying to do it all on my own, without any help from anyone—well, maybe, now and then, from my wife.

This led to a long conversation on why we were not very happy or satisfied. We sure as hell were busy enough, certainly cranking out some work which caught the attention of peers and colleagues, and we had also managed to create good homes. So . . . what was missing? Please don't get me wrong, we were not miserable or despairing, just naggingly aware we felt askew on some level of our being.

It is difficult for me to capture Manuel's voice or spirit. I am doing my best, but recognize we were such different personalities. He was tenaciously optimistic and positive, and I wore my heart on my sleeve, even when I was down or in the dumps. Still, there was no denying the time spent in recent years, discussing our wandering away from Life, or seemingly, to have lost a clear sense of direction—this was especially true in terms of adjusting to retirement.

In reviewing my notes, I felt we came up with three pretty clear and distinct answers as to what was missing, although there were a myriad number of candidates. Again, let me stress, we did not consider these seismic shifts in mood, but we did notice their incessant and ongoing presence—like the mosquito sound when it is in a holding pattern over our ear.

## MEANING

We both believed in what we were doing for a living, but we also felt a slow steady decline in its meaning for us. Personally speaking, we were less confident or hopeful. We deeply questioned if we were making any difference at all. We were growing more and more skeptical, as our culture seemed to be growing down rather than up.

The bottom line, we were both deeply doubting our overall sense of purpose, and were keenly aware we had far less reason to feel hopeful about the future. Since we both believed hope must be for everyone, everywhere, and for all time, we experienced our culture as lacking the maturity to advocate for a deep and **"WE-DRIVEN"** hope.

I believe our choice of the topic/theme of legacy for this manuscript reflects this search, and why we felt compelled to sift through what actually brought meaning to our lives, and what we wished to pass on to others.

We both still yearned for a clear vision and voice.

## MATURING

We truly questioned our own maturity. In our marriages and in our parenting. Careers. Friendships. Spiritual life. We wondered significantly about our fixation on people pleasing, performance, and perfection. We were weary a good deal of the time, and found ourselves often wanting to just escape, or get away from it all.

Even though Manuel's world had shrunk as his MS slowly progressed, it was still his, and the spiritual need to feel he mattered, was as robust in him as in me.

We both had come to believe that maturity and spirituality were like strands of DNA, and we could not pursue one without the other. Manuel's spiritual perspective was very careful, cautious, and even rigorous in not espousing any categorical or creedal styled beliefs. Manuel saw maturity as becoming a better and smarter individual, one wise to the ways of the world, while continuing to pay attention to one's ideals and hopes and dreams.

He made it clear he loved talking about spirituality and the soul, but did not have a need to come to any profound statements of faith. In fact, I knew Manuel would not sign-off on this book if it were to become too religious, or too personal—more of a memoir. This will not be the case, as I promised him, as I promise you, this is a non-religious book—while retaining a deeply spiritual perspective and edge.

My sense of maturity was truly linked to creating a hope for the future. It was fixated on the spirit and souls of our children and youth. I think we shared a conviction that we owed kids a quality hope, and could not claim to champion wisdom, if it did not include how to offer them ample hope for the future.

We both spoke of making concerted efforts to be adult mentors and friends to the young. We certainly put in a good deal of energy into this desire. Still, at present, we felt like those kids who go to a carnival, and then ride a spinning cylinder until it goes fast enough to glue them to the metal mesh walls, until the floor eerily gives way. Such a strange feeling, and so is this—not believing we really know how to offer our young people a genuine hope. Spinning like hell, but going nowhere.

We knew we needed to grow up. Not because we felt we were immature, but because our culture and times gave us such concern about the frequent expressions by today's youth, of their need and desire to witness real adult leadership.

We felt a need to build a stronger and deeper sense of courage, creativity, care, concern, and compassion. It was time to recognize our interdependence with the whole world, and the shrinking amount of time we had to address issues like the collapse of our climate, or the racial divisions which are again ripping us apart as a nation.

## MAKING A LIFE

We knew the point and purpose of Life could not possibly be just making a living. It could not be about gathering a big pile of stuff, or what we call, adult toys. It certainly could not be equated to how much money we had, or managed to save, or invest. Neither of us worshiped at Wall Street's doorstep. Both of us had deep ethical and moral concerns about what we experienced as capitalism out of control—void of any regulation to protect the all but forgotten public.

We were looking for substance, significance, and satisfaction. Ironically, we had come full circle back to where our spiritual search had first begun—what did our Higher Power hope for us today; what did God expect or wish from or for us?

We both were aware of what our culture expected and hoped for us, and recognized it was drastically different than what our souls longed for, or our spiritual growth required. Making a life cannot be about becoming more and more greedy. It is not about me ... me ... me. It is not about cluttering our lives and souls with more and more stuff, of less and less value; things with little longevity, and a smidgen of purpose.

We also knew we did not want our retirements to be about keeping ourselves entertained.

If we pursued meaning and maturity, we fully expected we could create a life not only of significance and substance, but one which daily offered us opportunities to serve, sacrifice, and make quality contributions to those around us, and to the world as a whole.

I think we both felt that in making a life, we must be grounded in the belief we are already enough—in all respects. Making a life is not about seeking the top rung on the ladder of success. It is the absence of all rungs, and a wish to receive each day as a blessing, and an attempt to live as a blessing as well.

Both of us would have contended that what was missing in our lives was threefold: 1) a lack of meaning, 2) disciplined maturity, and, 3) a clearer focus on making a life, rather than making a living. Up until the day Manuel died, it would be fair to say that our wandering away from Life on Life's terms, was rooted in these missing links.

## THE ART OF ACCEPTANCE

I have come to the belief, as did Manuel, that—the art of acceptance is critical. It is the very foundation of finding meaning, choosing to mature, and making a life worth the living. Acceptance is crucial for us to conclude that we are neither in charge, nor in control, and that Life asks us to surrender, to let go, and to receive. But acceptance and surrender are against the nature of our culture. The spiritual life is in direct opposition to the American way of life.

The American way is about achieving and accumulating and doing. The spiritual way is about receiving and embracing and being. The difference is enormous.

Acceptance is a long, arduous spiritual process. It is not about gaining something, but sacrificing our deep desire to be in control. It is coming to terms with what we know God, or a Higher Power, might wish for our lives. Acceptance means being willing to follow, because having done so has shown us a still better way: less cluttered and chaotic; less obsessed and stressed; and one which is at peace with our body and soul.

Acceptance is calling a truce, a genuine cease fire. It is to stop being at war with ourselves, others, or Life as a whole. Most of all, acceptance is finally waving the white flag, and knowing we truly just don't know; we do **NOT** have all the answers; we will get lost and lonely often; we need love and support and assistance, and on a daily basis. It is also the acceptance of aging and death, and the reality that we all will know our fair share of tragedy, sorrow, and loss—as well as serenity, satisfaction, and joy.

As a pastor for over forty years, I have watched so many marriages and families fall apart, simply due to an inability or an unwillingness to accept somebody for being who they truly are. Marriages are often wars of transformation, as one partner tries to clone the other. Families become badly divided, because, even though they may share a genetic code, members may still have vastly differing viewpoints, perspectives, behaviors, and yes, ethics and values and morals.

We do not inherit our souls. Our souls are influenced by our heritage and traditions, but will develop in their own unique way, buffered and bombarded by a litany of unique events and experiences. The soul is responsive to both nature and nurture, but also claims a decided openness to the presence of the Spirit, or a Higher Power.

The art of acceptance is often what is required in a genuine celebration of diversity. Manuel and I were such different people, and had such different expectations, wants, needs, even hopes and dreams. However, we accepted one another, and chose to celebrate our differences as the core of why our friendship was so strong and sturdy and intimate.

When I would apologize for talking too much, which was often, Manuel would always say, "Well, I need to talk more, and say what I truly think and feel and believe matters."

America has become a place and a people which is brutally intolerant of difference and often violently opposed to change of any kind. As a result, our culture is riddled by racism, sexism, ageism, and religious bigotry, as well as a refusal to admit when we are wrong. We can't acknowledge our own need to change, mature, grow, or admit to those times we obviously have failed to let ourselves be transformed by, or conformed to a Higher Power.

The Twelve Step Movement is anchored in a single premise—admitting we are powerless. In my mind, acceptance is also an admission of powerlessness, a release of one's grips, and the giving over of decisions to a God of our own interpretation. America is all about being powerful, in fact, power is our national obsession, and is at the root of the corruptness we witness in both politics and the Church.

Acceptance is an art. It takes discipline. It requires patience and perseverance. One can never get enough practice. An art is a craft, a making, a creating, a combination of work and Grace which yields a truly fine product. Any artist will tell you, be they a painter, a novelist, a poet, a woodcarver, a weaver, or a stained-glass maker, there is no possible way to try and be in control of the creative process. Creativity demands going with flow, following the Spirit, and trusting the final product not to be solely of our own design—it is created by the human spirit in consort with the Divine Spirit.

Acceptance is that point at which we relinquish our grip, ease the stress, allow our hands and heart to be open to reception, and free ourselves to follow our holy hunches and innate wishes. These are the moments when we lose track of time, sense another voice or vision, and can feel the presence of something deeply spiritual and whole and holy.

I have struggled mightily with the notion of writing this book without Manuel being present—unable to edit and critique. My acceptance came when I considered not doing it, letting the idea wither and die. Then I knew. Whatever this book may be, it will be enough, and I know Manuel will be present in it. I know he would have made edits and had critiques, even if I never know what they might have been. What I do know, is that he would be glad I gave it a shot.

Manuel would accept my writing of this manuscript, flaws and all. Trust me, I have paid close attention to Manuel's voice, and even as I write today, I can hear a comment he might make, an addition, a point of contention, or just an affirmation . . . or, simply saying, "Toss that!"

## WHAT ARE LIFE'S TERMS?

What are Life's terms? They are not like the Ten Commandments, chiseled into stone. They are definitely not about what NOT TO DO. Life's terms are about who to be, and what spirit to offer the world. Life's terms are not rocket science. They are simple, straightforward, and often quite obvious. They do not require several advanced degrees, but only some uncommon common sense.

My notes on Life's terms are considerable, written from conversations I had with Manuel, and showing a general consensus on most of the terms we eventually prioritized as our top Life terms. We came up with eight, each of equal importance, and our comfort level was uniform for each. They just made sense in our heads and hearts, and we knew our own lives had worked on keeping these terms—as best we could.

Again, remember this is not a list of suggested behaviors, like a diet plan, or a therapeutic program. It is simply a list of recommended attitudes, perspectives, and viewpoints, which we felt could facilitate our living out the will of God, or of our Higher Power, for our own lives.

Maybe you will want to change several terms on the list, or come up with a list of your own. We would applaud such an effort, and encourage putting your own personal stamp of approval on what you believe are Life's innate terms and conditions.

The key here is that these "terms" be human, universal, and in conformity to those spiritual programs or belief systems, which we have found honest, adult, and worthy of reflection.

The last thing on earth Manuel and I would have wanted is for our readers to interpret our list as a YOU MUST, YOU SHOULD,

OR YOU OUGHT TO DO IT OUR WAY. These are pointers, not dictums. They offer input, not a summation or proof. They are suggestions which we have learned to trust and offer them as such. We surrender them to you; we don't summon you to follow them, or know them by rote.

This list can be revised and shaped by others, which is as it should be, as it is the nature of any individual spiritual journey. Life is in flux, just as is our soul. The Spirit does not speak in dogma or doctrine, but offers a way, which if taken (which seldom happens), is likely to expose us to illuminating terms for our day to day lives.

## BEING ALIVE

Life requires us to be alive. This means to be awake, aware, and alert. If we are catatonic, numb, or dead before we are dead, we not only fail to mature, but we create nothing of value. Love also demands us to be fully alive, ready to receive, prepared to give, and offering everything we have in terms of caring, concern, and compassion.

Being alive asks us to embrace Life as a whole. This includes great mysteries, significant paradox, ample loss and tragedy, and of course, the formidable process of aging and dying. Life is difficult. It calls upon us to take risks, have dreams, make changes, and to become everything we believe we were meant by God, or our Higher Power, to be.

We were never meant to live in denial, under a bushel, detached, alienated, or in a fog. This is not living. This is surviving. Life is not meant to be an endurance test we cannot possibly pass. If we are to live according to Life's terms, then we must make a conscious decision to be fully alive. We must ask ourselves daily if we are ready to greet the day with open eyes, heart, soul, and spirit, ready to experience all of its rituals, peculiarities, troubles, and triumphs.

(In spite of living with MS for over forty years, Manuel still managed to crank out a most robust life. He often regretted how he felt his mind could be clouded or untrustworthy because of the disease, but I would say, in his wrestling match with MS, it was the disease which usually got pinned.)

## BEING HUMAN

It is the will of God for humans to be human. Sadly, many of us spend our entire lives trying to be anything but human. We play God. We become robots or automatons. We let ourselves become characters wearing masks, make-up, costumes, and playing a role which has little to do with the longings of our own soul.

Being a human means we make mistakes, we have flaws, we flop, we fail, and we can be first-class fools. It also means we are capable of outstanding courage and heroism. We are capable of life-saving compassion and concern, monumental creativity and the actualization of outrageous dreams. We can achieve a willingness to take risks on behalf of what we believe, love, and care passionately about — OUR ULTIMATE CONCERNS.

The choice is ours. These choices will create our legacy. Are we aware of the legacy we are creating? This was the impetus for this entire manuscript; Manuel asking me if I had any idea how I wished to be remembered. It was a haunting question then and it remains one now. I hope it will be a true challenge for you the reader as well, and one which inspires you to create a legacy that is lasting and laced with love.

Manuel was more comfortable in his own skin; more at home with his own soul; and more at ease with Life on Life's terms, than literally anyone I have ever known.

## BEING HONEST

Life depends on our being honest and consistently on the up and up. Lying does not create; it can only destroy. Ultimately, every lie has the potential to be destructive and evil. Even the smallest fib, a white lie, an exaggeration, a fabrication, all have the potential to slowly become sinister. Yes, we all tell them, a lie or two or three, and a few whoppers along the way, but if it becomes a habit, pattern, and worse, a strategy for rearranging reality to suit our needs, then it has become dangerous.

Manuel felt quite strongly it was time in our culture, to ask ourselves how our children were being impacted by the gross level of lying, deceit, distortion, exaggeration, and fabrication in our society. He suspected the influence was substantial, corrosive to their maturing, and a sad subtle force which brought out the worst in us, and thus, in our youth.

We both seriously wondered if we might actually be creating a generation of kids who felt it was perfectly fine to lie, to make it up as you go along, or create some conspiracy theory to cover your tracks. We had no idea how our youth were being influenced by those in our culture who cannot admit or accept defeat. A nation of sore losers would be truly pathetic, and a deep wound on our nation's honor and heart.

I never experienced Manuel telling a lie, exaggerating or embellishing, or ever being even remotely mean-spirited or unkind. He was gracious of heart and mind, and had a most gentle spirit. His words were really quite pure and true.

## BEING REAL

A long, long time ago, Coca Cola spent a good sum of money to find out what was the most important word to the American teenager. After substantial investigation, and polling of all kinds, it was determined the single word which mattered most to our youth was—REAL; and so, Coke became the REAL THING. Ironic, to say the least.

I think the concept of REAL still matters to our youth. However, I doubt they have as firm a grasp on the concept now, anymore, than they had back then. There are so many factors at play in America today, factors which encourage and enable our youth to choose to be artificial and image addicted. There is little in our culture which actually encourages us to be authentic or original.

Think of it this way. We live in a culture which brags about offering the good life, knowing full well our lifestyles seldom seem focused on anything having to do with goodness. Our greedy, celebrity-driven culture has no real desire to be true to its convictions and would likely be hard pressed to even name those convictions.

If we are to come back to Life on Life's terms, however, we will be required to be the real deal. We must be original, honest and true, authentic, the genuine article. Above all, we need the integrity to say what we mean and mean what we say, as well as living out those values we cherish and pass on. If Life's terms call upon us to be mature, then we must never be a fraud or a fake, and must always be trustworthy, honorable, and leave a legacy full of genuine truths.

Manuel was the real thing in the deepest and truest sense of those words; not a phony bone in his body. Trust me, I can be judgmental, unfortunately, but I cannot think of anything I ever experienced Manuel say or do or be, which I would have labeled as fake.

## BEHOLD

Life asks us to behold the beauty and grandeur and glory of Creation. Life also asks us to be held in an embrace of Grace. Life's intention is to move us to higher ground, so we can see further, get the big picture, and envision an even better tomorrow.

Most people find it impossible to behold Nature, and not sense the presence of God or a Higher Power. Chasing beauty is a key aspect of our calling. We are compelled to look, listen, taste, touch, and smell the wonders of Nature. We are also asked to know what comes naturally to us, and is our second nature. Those talents, gifts, and attributes are equally vital to our calling.

We all have a calling, but not to a career. We may be lucky enough to have a job or career for which we are well equipped and suited, but our true calling is simply to be so alive, so honest and human and real, that we can behold our Higher Power. When we do, we gain an understanding of a God, and we come to celebrate the sacredness of everything on this earth, and every moment within each day.

Manuel so loved those days when he could sit outside, enjoy the sun, see the sky, feel a breeze, or notice a bird or flower or even a butterfly. If this sounds like a damn Hallmark card, too bad—it was the truth and the whole truth and nothing but the truth, so help me God.

## BELOVED

Our God, or our Higher Power, or the Spirit or Power we might call Divine, feels only love for us, and does so unconditionally and incessantly. In the eyes of God, we are always enough. More than enough. We are whole and holy. Not holier than thou, but of such goodness as to be worthy of being called God's own children.

Manuel felt most beloved when with his wife and daughter. They were his home and his now and his heaven.

## BE SIGNIFICANT

Manuel and I discussed success a lot. We felt it was our culture's obsession, and was equated to money, stuff, fame, power, and notoriety. We both came to feel it was an unworthy goal in terms of legacy.

Legacy was about being significant. Being significant was about making a difference, but doing so modestly. No crazed ambition, no pursuit of money. Significance is to live a life which is memorable, even unforgettable. A life of significance focuses on love, mercy, service, sacrifice, substance, and standing up for those suffering or in need. A significant life champions causes which seek to lift up the despairing or lost.

A soul of significance is not self-focused. Significance demands, instead, that we be people of integrity, dignity, maturity, authenticity, as well as gracious and extravagant in loving and forgiving.

Are we pursuing a way of life which will enable us to leave a legacy of significance? This is a great and essential spiritual question to ask ourselves. Pursuing this line of inquiry can ignite a good life, and one which will help inspire us to make the world a better place in which to live. We long for a simpler, saner, far more serene, more deeply spiritual world.

Manuel was of great significance to all who knew him—even just slightly.

> *A life of significance focuses on love, mercy, service, sacrifice, substance, and standing up for those suffering or in need. A significant life champions causes which seek to lift up the despairing or lost.*

## BEWARE

Life comes with its own warning labels.

We are daily being told this Earth is precious, and fragile, and how we must work with diligence and dedication to keep it in proper balance.

Our climate is offering us the flashing red lights of wildfires, monster storms, severe droughts, and a growing lack of water. Time is running out. Many experts feel we have already passed the point of no return and the damage done is irreparable.

Extinction hovers in the back of everyone's minds, and on the forefront for many of our youth.

We listen to the hate and verbal hostility throughout our culture. Racism and bigotry are now out in the open, and they appear to be gaining strength. How is a nation, so deeply engrained in Judeo-Christian values, willing to think or believe only white people are precious in the sight of God?

Women are saying, "ME TOO," to make it clear they have had enough of being thought of as sexual objects or pieces of meat. They will no longer be seen as servers and pleasurers of men, especially men of power.

The gap between the rich and poor is obscene and it only widens and worsens. What does God think of a Third World? What about a millionaire or a billionaire, or someone who can take their own rocket on a pleasure trip into space—just a thrilling outing, no matter what the cost? Such an expense might add up to the GNP of several of those Third World countries.

Violence is being encouraged as if all should be armed or that a noble purpose exists in owning an assault weapon, other than killing other human beings. What is next? If we feel a need for a bazooka or a tank or a bomb, then this is our right? Wrong.

Greed remains America's primary and deepest spiritual issue. Greed keeps us from maturing and fuels our power-hungry rage, hatred, lack of empathy or compassion. Greed is the subtle creation of evil in all facets of our culture.

We refuse to celebrate diversity or equality, and we offer little hope of making peace in our world and in our times.

Yes... there are many acts of human kindness. So many good folks doing good things and being good people. So many amazing efforts to save the Creation, to keep the Earth livable for all and for all time. There is still a tremendous presence of love and mercy and generosity and graciousness.

But... there are some glaring and frequent warning signs as well, and we must take heed. We must stand up, fight back, work harder, care more, take risks, and still dream of a world as One. Our ideals matter, as do our stories, and our lives. We know we can do better than we are doing.

America is certainly no longer the moral leader of the world, and this bothered Manuel and I a great deal. It truly did.

Manuel struggled until the day he died, to understand how Americans of any legitimate faith, could find it in their hearts and souls, to take children away from parents, and then house them in modified kennels or cages, and see this crazy wall as a moral declaration of our greatness.

## AN OLD-FASHIONED GENTLEMAN

I have said this before, Manuel was in many ways, a truly old-fashioned gentleman. I hesitate to refer to him this way, in case this is heard as describing him as out of date, not contemporary or modern, or worse, part of an establishment aristocracy, where gentlemen were often found to be tyrants behind closed doors, good manners just for show, kind gestures just images. They resembled biblical folks who always tried to pray in public places—so they could be seen.

I only knew my grandfather, Einar Hjortness, until I was seven, when he died suddenly of a heart attack. Still, I always thought he was just the nicest, sweetest guy, and he always made me feel like a million bucks.

He affirmed me and told me my mother was one of the finest women who ever walked. He winked at me, and told me that someday I might meet someone as wise and wonderful and beautiful as my Grandmother. He never bragged. He never bad mouthed anyone. I heard him say a few cuss words, but they were in Danish, so I didn't pay much attention.

The summer he died he took me to a baseball game at Douglas Park. He convinced my mother I would be safe, even if we were outside after the streetlights had come on. He told me we would have popcorn and a Coke, and that I could yell at the umps, as long as I did not get carried away.

It was fast pitch softball, and the game featured the two top teams in Racine . . . Andis Clipper versus Merchant's Delivery. I screamed and yelled and cheered my lungs out, and Grandpa just laughed at me, and called me a "corker."

In the seventh inning we got in line for our popcorn and Coke. A little Italian lady with a heavy accent worked in a metal shed, doling out candy bars and popsicles and cups of Borden's ice Cream, as well as our choice—heavily buttered popcorn in small grease-stained brown bags, and green six-ounce bottles of Coke.

While we waited, a Merchant's Delivery Truck pulled up and unloaded a large Coca Cola red and white cooler. The little Italian lady was delighted, jumping up and down, and yelling, "It is here! It is here!"

My grandfather explained to me that the cooler meant the little Italian lady would no longer have to have big blocks of ice by her feet, to keep things cold. The cooler would be so much more convenient for her, and this was important, because she was such a hard worker.

When the Merchant's delivery man asked the little Italian lady for $41.00, she screamed and sobbed, "Too much. Too much. You only a come a couple blocks. Just a couple. Too much. I no make that in a week."

My grandfather told me to stay put and to keep our place in line. When he left me there, I was frightened and furious. I intended to tell my mom he had abandoned me. That was for sure.

I could see my grandfather had removed his Sam Sneed hat. He wore it every single day of the summer and was passing it among the fans on both sides of the infield. In no more than five minutes, he returned with his hat stuffed with fives and ones, and maybe a lone ten.

He walked up to the men who drove the truck, and he said, "Here is your money boys, and five extra bucks for doing such important work. You see this lovely lady here makes the best popcorn on the planet, and we could not possibly think of watching a game at Douglas Park, without her popping up some of her magic."

With that, the line applauded, and the little Italian woman gave us free popcorn and Cokes, and me a Borden's cup of vanilla; she scooted out from the shed, and kissed my red-faced Grandfather on the cheek.

On the way home, Grandpa told me it was important to value everybody's work and to help out workers when they needed it. He said President Roosevelt taught all Americans to be good neighbors, and to make sacrifices, and share. He said nobody should ever be as rich as a Rockefeller, as nobody was that much better than anyone else. He always told me how finding oil was not even close to the importance of being a good teacher or a hard worker—like the little Italian lady.

I never ever forgot that night.

When he died, my mother told me he was a genuine gentleman. He was so kind and caring and good. She was so proud to be his daughter. I told her I understood, but I didn't.

Only much later, did I fully comprehend his quiet dignity, his fierce Socialist beliefs, and his allegiance to all things public. Only when I was an adult myself, did I recognize what he had done that night, for a little Italian lady, and for his grandson, who he wanted to know—"Billy, everyone deserves a free lunch now and then, that is why God put us on this earth . . . to help each other out . . . make Life a little easier . . . and lift folks up when they are down."

Manuel was this kind of gentleman. His values were decidedly old-fashioned and yet so amazingly progressive in soul and spirit. My grandfather was unforgettable. So was Manuel. I suspect, they shared a similar view of Life, and how neighbors must treat neighbors, and what satisfaction kindness can bring.

There are times in Life when we must go back before we can go forward. Times when we must recognize there are pieces of the past worthy of being retrieved and retooled. It is wise to be aware of when the good old days were better, and then ask why; and then see if we might bring those old values and ethics into our present.

> "Coming back is the thing that enables you to see how all the dots in your life are connected, how one decision leads you to another, how one twist of fate, good or bad, brings you to a door that later takes you to another door, which aided by several detours—long hallways and unforseen stairwells—eventually put you in the place you are now.
> –Ann Patchett

> "Joy is not just about being happy. Joy is a rigorous spiritual practice of saying yes to life on life's terms."
> –Mark Matousek

# Lesson Four:

# "PREJUDICE CAN BE CRIPPLING"

"To live anywhere in the world today and be against equality because of race or color is like living in Alaska and being against snow.
–William Faulkner

"Prejudice is a disease characterized by hardening of the categories."
–William Arthur

"Every bigot was once a child free of prejudice."
–Sister Mary de Lourdes

*Dear Readers,*

*I need to ask your indulgence at this point in the manuscript.*

*This is a chapter which addresses the hot potato topics of prejudice, bigotry, and racism. These are also topics which deeply impacted Manuel's life—including his wife and daughter, mother and father, and four siblings.*

*Manuel knew prejudice firsthand. He also had some real regrets in this arena, namely not having spoken up enough. Manuel found prejudice, bigotry, and racism, collectively, to be a cancer on America's soul. He believed it was crippling to us as a culture and as a people.*

*Manuel spoke often of the high level of denial on this topic, and how he found white folks unable to name and claim the bigotry he witnessed in their lives. He stated it was like knowing someone with an addiction, who just could not go the whole distance, and say, "This is my problem, and I need to do something about it and make some changes."*

*Manuel deeply regretted not having been a strong, fierce, fervent, and incessant voice in battling prejudice, bigotry, and systemic racism in America. He hoped a significant piece of his legacy would be to have been a real fighter for equality, diversity, and inclusion. He told me he too often had been too quiet, civil, even shy, when it came to addressing this complex social issue.*

*Manuel felt some real guilt that he had played it way too safe.*

*I do not want this manuscript to add to Manuel's guilt or silence. I hope to make it abundantly clear where he stood on these important cultural and moral issues. Manuel had deep core values on the subject and he was passionate about the need to uproot all forms of racism. He was fully committed to celebrating equality, and seeking to transform human hearts, from callus cruel prejudice and bigotry into souls of compassion and concern.*

*I would contend that Manuel was neither prejudiced nor a bigot, though he had just cause to be. If you knew him, then I think you would agree. Racism was also not a personal habit he battled, but it was a potent cultural and political force with which he often had to contend. Again, it is not my intention or desire to paint Manuel as a person without flaw, but I am stating what I experienced—I never knew him to judge anyone.*

*I agree with Manuel's assessment, however, that his silence on these subjects was due to his shyness, his desire to be civil and kind at all times, and a habit learned from a father who only spoke up when in the com-*

*pany of other Hispanics. Manuel could have said more, and I wish he had, but I accept why that just did not often happen.*

*I genuinely hope he died knowing no shame or guilt. The life he lived celebrated equality and diversity as well as anyone could ever have imagined doing.*

*I ask you to read this chapter NOT through the lens of your own political views, but embrace its contents, as a chance to get to know a great individual a little bit better. Please, do not judge. Simply absorb and consider the convictions expressed. Please know how deeply Manuel cared about these issues in our nation and our world.*

*Sincerely,*
*Bill Grimbol*

Let me begin by stating the obvious. There is no humility to be found in prejudice. None. Not a drop. Not an ounce.

This manuscript focuses on how humility is the foundation upon which we build good lives and how some of us may attain greatness in the eyes of others.

Humility was the attitude and perspective which saturated Manuel Barrera's whole being, and became the core of his character, and the essence of his spirit.

Manuel did come to discern the deep wounds and scars created by prejudice and bigotry. He had witnessed it. He had heard it. He had experienced it. From childhood to adulthood, racism orbited his life, and landed more often than he first imagined. The racism in America was deep, with agonizingly tangled roots, and systemic, in every facet of our society.

We both concluded how in America, we needed to name and claim the bigotry which infested our souls, and the souls of so many of our fellow citizens. Racism is like ground water, and it ends up seeping into everything. If the water is polluted, well pollution spreads slowly but surely.

Bigotry is expressed in a multiplicity of evil ways—the KKK, the Proud Boys, any and all white supremacist movements or organizations. It can be subtle, like a bad joke, or a racial slur, but in recent months, it has found its footing. Racism is now being sanctioned in America, and this has unleashed a rank stench wafting about our entire culture.

It became clear to both of us that America was still mired in the same wicked racism, which had spawned the Civil War. In this chapter, I wish to explore my many conversations with Manuel on prejudice, bigotry, and racism in America. Several of these were quite recent, and some all the way back to the seventh grade at Washington Junior High School.

Let me start there—back in the seventh grade.

There was a new student in the seventh grade. He was a Native American. To this very day, I do not know his name—but he was called "Chief" by everyone. His hair was never combed, he wore the same clothes almost every day, with perhaps a change of T-shirt, and he was always laughing. He even laughed when people punched him, slapped him on the back of the head, or shoved him down the stairs.

Chief never spoke. He could speak, he just chose not to. His was the presence of an awkward, pure silence. He must have thought his silence would protect him or enable him to disappear. It did neither.

One day in gym class, for some completely unknown or fabricated reason, they pushed him down the locker room stairs, pulled off his pants and underwear, and pounded his head against the wall. Still smiling, he slumped to the floor and began to weep. Then he passed out.

The "they" were the ninth-grade boys, and "they" were indeed into power. They had almost full control. Every boy in the school knew it. I believe every teacher or administrator did as well.

When Coach Ford ran over, and saw the blood trickling from the back of Chief's head, he began to scream, "Who did this? Tell me right now, who the hell did this?" Again, silence ruled the day.

About a month later, Manuel and I noticed that Chief was gone. We went to Coach Ford and asked where he had gone. We told Coach, we would be glad to try to befriend him if he could come back.

"Thank you boys, I am proud to hear you say that, but the administration feared for that boy's life. I cannot tell you where he is, but he is safe. We made sure of that. What happened here was a disgrace, and it will be corrected."

Manuel and I noticed that even Coach Ford did not seem to know Chief's real name and that Chief was spoken of as if he were a thing or object, now kept in a "safe" of some kind.

Then Manuel said to me, "That could have been me, Bill, that could have been me."

I told Manuel he was nuts, and I reminded him he was the most popular boy in our class. He told me that to some of the older guys, he was just another greasy spic. He made it clear, how under the right conditions, if he were found alone, or mouthed off, or called one of them a name, he could have met the same fate.

"Bill, don't you see? A lot of the time I am just like Chief. I smile most of the time. I stay out of the way and quiet. I seldom open my mouth. I just happen to be a good student and athlete and my mother makes sure I wear clean clothes. Trust me. I always know. It could have been me. If I were just a shade browner, Bill. Just another shade darker."

When I got home from school, my mom was making burgers at the stove and I told her everything that happened to Chief and everything Manuel had said.

I noticed she was weeping and I asked her why. She told me it was because Manuel was right. It could have been him. "Nobody deserves the treatment Chief got. I hate that we don't even know his name. I am going to find out that boy's name if it is the last thing I do."

Now, sixty years later—Chief remains anonymous. My mother actually made over twenty calls. Her efforts were rebuked with confidentiality as the reason. She so ached for Chief though she never met the boy. Her compassion was real and full.

Prejudice is evil. Evil is void of all empathy, and prejudice is reflective of having no empathy for the targeted group. Prejudice is a bias. It is a judgment without merit. It is the need to push someone else down, while pushing ourselves up. Prejudice is grounded in ignorance. It has no desire to know the Truth. It is bloated with the malignant pride of thinking oneself superior over another.

"A prejudice is a vagrant opinion without visible means of support."
–Ambrose Bierce

Prejudice is an incessant belittling, the actual destruction of another human being's self-esteem. The prejudice of those who believe they have all the answers, or consider themselves to be innately better than others will continue to grow. This prejudice will fill with the infection of hate, and be expressed through more and more violence—verbally, physically, and deeply.

> "Too many of our prejudices are like pyramids upside down.
> They rest on tiny, trivial incidents, but they spread
> upward and outward until they fill our minds."
> –William McChesney Martin

Manuel spoke quietly of America being a nation swarming with racial prejudice, bigotry, and in recent years, a venomous hate. He spoke with significant passion about those Americans "incarcerated" on reservations; a Wall being built near his home, which he considered a moral abomination; the savage separation of children from their migrant parents; and the housing of these kids in what he called "kennel camps." From Manuel's perspective, these incidents were collectively a national disgrace.

Manuel often said he truly believed there was just cause to arrest many of our government officials, all the way to the top, for child abuse. I knew he meant it, as his voice became, well, not loud, but firm, even fierce.

As I previously acknowledged, Manuel often referred to his father's dual life. How his dad was an articulate, witty, charming, charismatic leader when within the Hispanic community, but when in the company of whites, he became a shy, quiet, hapless, hopeless, quite empty-seeming man.

In our more recent conversations, Manuel was able to admit how he saw some of his oft praised humility, as really a choice of security, and a problem-free ticket to pursue his dreams. He talked of how many white folks, even while he was studying for his Ph.D., were looking for any chance to poke the bubble of his dream.

He also told me how my own mother had worked hard to show Manuel she was not prejudiced in any way. As a means of compensating for her guilt, she would make him steak and homemade French fries when he stayed over—and always kissed him good night. We both laughed, and Manuel said he was secretly glad she felt guilty—he loved the steak and fries, and even the kiss on the forehead.

Manuel once said to me, "Well, Bill, white folks have one hell of a lot to feel guilty about."

This time I was the silent one. I agreed then, and I do now, in fact, even more so today. I told Manuel on several occasions, that my soul swarmed with shame, as I truly began to understand the scope of racism in America. I admitted my belief to him, that a tremendous number of white folks harbor genuine fascist views; they believe themselves to be innately superior to people of color.

We whites know we have a clear advantage. No matter what we say, we know we have the upper hand. This power and special treatment is addictive. It is also a spiritual disease, just like any other addiction. It is also an elitism, an unspoken caste system, and the creator of untold stories of bias and brutality. The white preference for a "whites only" political and social system, or set of values, is an ongoing tragedy of our culture and its history.

I recall telling Manuel, there was not a white church (there weren't more than a handful of white churches?? Being hopeful here) in America, that would choose a black or brown or red or yellow pastor, unless forced. The Church sings of Jesus loving all the little children, but America's Jesus clearly seems to love white children a little bit more—maybe quite a bit more. It was painful to admit and spiritually nauseating, but it was a truth I have had to face, and one which Manuel has had to cope with every single day.

Far too many white Christians are quite comfortable claiming to believe in Jesus, while remaining blatant bigots. I find it so ironic to attend Presbytery meetings and listen to clergy and elders debate the ordination of gay men and women. They seem to have no such concerns or questions about ordaining bigots. We have more bigoted elders than anyone could know or count.

I once told Manuel about a black professor I had at Princeton Theological Seminary. Edler Hawkins told us at the start of every single class—the most segregated hour in America is on Sunday morning. This always got our attention and focused us on a monumental task—how could we expel prejudice and racism from the Church? Nothing has changed.

I find the recent surge of racism, the sprouting up of many neo-Nazi groups, and the growing number of white supremacy-centered groups to be alarming. It orbits the soul of America every day and it threatens to paralyze our capacity to function as a democracy. It keeps us from being people who believe America is still a melting pot.

It leaves us wondering, where do we go from here? How can we possibly free ourselves from a force so deeply rooted, a system which gets more tangled and knotted by the day? At best, we must try to work on the problem, and first by acknowledging it is **OUR** problem. We must admit it is every American's, and that it is indeed a major issue. We also need to face the harsh reality, the prophetic vision, of fascism having come to America.

We must do something, and here are a few suggestions of where to begin. Yes, I know, begin again . . . and again . . . and again . . . until it becomes a habit, and the habit a hope.

## ASK THE TOUGH QUESTIONS

We desperately need to ask ourselves some difficult questions. Am I a bigot? Am I prejudiced? Am I a racist? What about my family, my extended family, and my family history?

If I am white, do I have any friends of color? Have I been inside their homes, or they, mine? Do I shop or eat or have a drink at any establishment I know to be run by a person of color?

Do I tend to politically affiliate with candidates who share my prejudices, or to those who ask me to mature and disown such bigotry?

How do I tend to blame or judge people of color?

Why do so many white Americans lump people of color into one amorphous mass, as if they are of like mind, beliefs, and behaviors?

Would I feel comfortable if my child were to marry a person of color?

Would I be okay with my child attending a school where there is a large, or even equal, minority population?

Do you believe there are some states or sections of the USA, which are more racist than others? Why?

Do you believe God made whites superior?

Could an Auschwitz or Buchenwald ever be created here? Why or why not?

Do you feel the justice system heavily favors white defendants? Why?

Why are our prisons so heavily populated with men and women of color?

We whites need to come clean with ourselves, and this means to answer the tough questions truthfully. We need to be brutally honest about our racial prejudices, particular biases, or bigoted views. We need to take a long hard look as to why it is that white supremacy movements have cost millions upon millions of lives.

It is time for us white folks to take stock. Enough bigoted jokes and comments and racial slurs. Enough with remaining quiet when witness to racist or bigoted attacks. Enough of working politically to keep people of color away from power, wealth, voting, or being elected.

Manuel and I had a friendship built on a foundation of asking such tough questions. It deepened our friendship. We shared a remarkably high level of openness, honesty, and intimacy. Our questioning and friendship offered us both a measure of hope and purpose. Our discussions in preparation for writing a book together were so probing. We explored our own personal and professional motivations and carefully examined the nature of what was truly happening within our culture.

It was so powerful. This book, much of it written in tribute and as a remembrance, is so worthy of completion, even with the obvious missing piece. It is that hole, which in many respects will make it somewhat holy. If we claim to care about Manuel, respect him, and wish to honor him, we can do so by recognizing the vital importance of working against racism or bigotry of any kind.

## STOP JUDGING

One effective strategy to address these issues in America, is to work spiritually to STOP judging others.

Mother Teresa wisely noted that when we are judging someone, we cannot love them.

Ralph Waldo Emerson pointed out that what we often call sin in others, we call experimentation in ourselves.

Mark Twain joked effectively about the urgent call for the reform of other people's bad habits.

I would add how any wisdom to be shed on this situation or subject is made null and void by being judgmental.

Striving not to be judgmental is a simple spiritual strategy, and one which has a proven history of lowering the levels of bigotry and prejudice and racism. When we actually do love our neighbor as ourself, we both become better people.

"Judge not" is a smart way to start the day and gives wisdom the wiggle room it might need to make some headway on the issue.

I remind our readers that I never . . . and I do mean never . . . heard Manuel judge another human being. I am not saying he never did, but I am telling you I never observed or heard it. I on the other hand, well . . .

## THE RISK OF INCLUSION

As a youth minister, I faced one particular problem in every church I served. Most of the parents wanted there to be an active youth program for the "good kids" of the church. They all assumed their own children were "good kids".

I always wished to recruit some of our troubled youth, the difficult youth, the tough-to-love youth, too. This was uniformly frowned upon. It was a battle for all forty plus years of my working with teens.

I understood. Parents feared for their kids. They did not relish the idea of their young sons or daughters brushing shoulders with those youth they found suspect, scary, or a misfit. Trust me when I say, most of the youth who attended, including the "good kids," drank, did some drugs, and were sexually active. However, many parents were absolutely certain their child "would never do that," and their child "would always tell them the truth."

One thing I know about teenagers is they are masters at living double lives. What parents think is going on is about 10% of what is actually occurring. Now, with the rampant advancement of technology, our youth have access to creating a "world" that most parents, and pastors, can't even begin to comprehend.

All teens are troubled at times. The youth I am most concerned for, in terms of becoming suicidal or depressed, are those referred to as being too good to be true—they are just that, too good to be true; their soul or heart is often in hiding.

Manuel and I experienced work with a wide range of adolescents. Some were quite sophisticated, had powerful, positive, and productive images, and were destined to know a good deal of societal success.

Most teens, or adults, could walk into any high school, spend the day wandering about, having lunch, and talking in the halls, and by the end of the day, tell you who would be on the Homecoming Court for King and Queen.

Other adolescents come with obvious issues. They are homely. They are poor. They are way too fat or short or skinny or tall. They have bad teeth, acne, or a lazy eye. Almost anything during adolescence can become a bold badge of dishonor.

Then there are those kids who clearly are troubled, struggling with self-esteem, anxiety, sexual orientation or activity. Some cope with homes filled with abuses of all kinds, from alcoholism to volatile divorces and incest. They have a darkness within them. They always seem sad or mad or bad. These teens are worriers, and they worry us.

If we are to address the issues that can be found in every high school in America, and empathize with our adolescent population, we need to get rid of the notion of "good kids" and "bad kids." We need to recognize that adolescence is a disturbed and stress-filled time.

There is the reality of an identity crisis. There is trying to fall in love or be loved by someone other than one's family. There is the hefty task of declaring one's independence, when most teens have never admitted their dependence.

Add to this variety pack of youth, those who are addicted, show signs of mental illness, or have been abused in some way, and the picture can get pretty bleak. What makes it all even worse is the foolishness of parents and teachers and administrators endorsing this crazy notion of the great divide—the "good kids" and the "bad kids."

A huge area of prejudice in America is our willingness to label certain kids as "bad" long before they have had a chance to sort anything out.

Parents can be unconsciously, extraordinarily bigoted as to who they find to be worthy or unworthy of association with their own children.

The downward slide of public schools is the direct result of racism. It is disturbing to see so many primarily white private or Christian schools, who just happen to have several black or brown athletes on their teams. It is wrong, and unfair, and we all do know what is going on.

Manuel and I had a deep devotion to the concept of a public school. In Racine we attended good schools with great teachers and learned to function within a student body which was diverse. We are now seeing these same public schools becoming primarily for students of color. The white exodus to rural schools, private schools, and a great number of Christian schools, is glaring and deeply troubling.

Public education, along with public health, transportation, and assistance, are all home to systemic racism. As a culture, we need to massively support all things public, and become less obsessed with all things private. Our children need to know WE is of far greater importance and value than just ME.

Inclusion will never be easy. There is nothing we tend to respond to with a greater array of excuses and defenses, as we do the denial of someone being part of our group or clan.

In the past few years, I have spoken to several parents of youth from Shelter Island. They often speak of their shock at how many white adolescent boys have gotten involved with white Aryan literature on the internet. I am shocked by their shock. Fascism is a global issue, and, once again, it is already on our shores in a big way.

These are evil times. We are not only deeply divided, but almost half of us do not see inclusion as one of the goals to which our democracy has long ascribed.

"Nothing dies too hard, or rallies so often, as intolerance."
–Henry Ward Beecher

## NO LONGER NEUTRAL

"If you are neutral in situations of injustice,
you have chosen the side of the oppressor."
–Desmond Tutu

In working on the outline for this book, Manuel asked me a most interesting question. "If I were to attend Horlick High School today, what would I experience? What would the differences be? How have the times changed at our former high school?"

To be honest, we both felt uncertain, as we had not been back in years. We also knew it was of no help to think the worst, or to be harshly judgmental. So, we tried to think about the basics of high school, and what Manuel, as a Hispanic male of ample talent and good looks, might experience today.

I have decided to write only about Manuel's speculations, and not my own. I felt they were worthy of greater attention, and they would yield something far more productive. I cannot quote Manuel on this one, but I can lift up five differences he believed he would have noticed if he were a student at Horlick today.

1. There would be a great many more students of color. He thought they would be less inclusive as a group, and far tighter with those of "their own kind."

2. Students of color would be angrier, far more aware of the glaring unfairness and racism of our culture. He cited an atmosphere of tension and stress, and students of color being more vigilant in not being treated with prejudice or bias.

3. He would not have many, if any, white friends. His social life would be predominantly, if not exclusively, with other Hispanic students. He felt it highly unlikely he would befriend any black students. He would likely date only Hispanic girls.

4. He would **NOT** be thought of as one of the "good Mexicans", or being "more white acting", and Manuel confessed to wondering how this may have impacted his overall development, experience, and soul.

5. He would stand up and speak up more often, and be an advocate for racial justice, putting an end to bigotry, and preventing prejudice in all forms. He would be less passive or in hiding. He would talk honestly about the experience of being Hispanic in America, in Racine, and at Horlick.

I joked with him that he sounded like A REBEL WITH A CAUSE. He said this would be what he would hope, as he felt he would be empowered by the large Hispanic population at Horlick today, and he would be called by a modern culture so clearly far off course, so rooted in prejudice and bigotry, and so unwilling to claim our history of systemic racism. He said it was not the time or place to deny or pretend.

Manuel felt he would likely still be a good student and athlete, but that chasing girls, and even looking for some trouble, would be on his radar screen. He spoke with real enthusiasm, and he sounded as though this thought alone made him happy. His world would have been wider, deeper, fuller, more honest, human, and actively striving to create hope.

Most of all, Manuel sounded colorful. No longer mainly taupe. No longer restrained or conformist. He was no longer giving his impression of Switzerland—a small neutral nation. Manuel sounded, in his fantasy at least, as somebody who came alive. He made it clear how being proud of being Hispanic, being invested in the Hispanic community, its politics and longings and needs, would demand someone of greater courage and creativity.

I think the fantasy itself was exciting and energizing for Manuel.

I was shocked when I found out Manuel had preached numerous times at his home church in Racine. I had no idea of this interest, talent, or passion. It led me to wonder, what kind of sermon he would have delivered on the topic of prejudice, bigotry, and racism today. I can guarantee you, he would have been prophetic, challenging, pointed, honest, and yet, still led by the spirit of Grace.

One thing is for sure, he would not have seen silence and cowering as the response of a man or woman of faith. He would have called upon his flock to climb up to higher ground, where equality was the norm, and diversity the expectation. He would have been courageous this time around; less a people pleaser or performer; less worried about his image or reputation.

This time, he would have led, been a mover and a shaker, but of the spiritual kind. I can see it. I can hear it. I really can.

"I refuse to accept the view that mankind is so tragically bound to the starless midnight of racism and war that the bright daybreak of peace and brotherhood can never become a reality... I believe that unarmed truth and unconditional love will have the final word."
–Dr. Martin Luther King, Jr.

Prejudice is an enormous burden on the soul of America, a weight upon our heart and our hope. It is confusing, disorienting, and creates a fog through which we cannot see our past. It is a major threat to the future of our planet and the longings and yearnings of our people. It hides the present behind walls, dividing lines, and camouflage of all kinds.

Prejudice impacts us all and for all time. It can cause permanent damage and rob us of our soul, both as a nation and as individuals. Prejudice can prevent us from caring, creating, or maturing, and leave us empty, hollow, with Life on hold.

Prejudice is crippling, because it is so vile and insidious. It spreads like an ink stain and, like that stain, is hard to remove. Prejudice is demonic in nature and evil in spirit. Like an automatic weapon, it has no other function but to destroy lives.

I believe Manuel's experience of growing up in Racine was dramatically different than my own, simply because he was forced to grapple with the rigidity and vise-like grip of prejudice. It shaped his days and clearly altered his dreams.

This still makes me sad. Sad that I did not know the name of "Chief" and did nothing. Sad that I called Manuel my best friend, but on the whole, still did nothing.

I have regrets. I have some guilt. I am aware that the white hatred of people of color is not only dangerous, but also damning. We continue to foster such attitudes and behaviors at our own peril.

# Lesson Five:

# "BE HUMBLE"

"Humility is not thinking less of yourself, it's thinking of yourself less."
–C.S. Lewis

"None are so empty as those who are full of themselves."
–Benjamin Whichcote

"Lord, when we are wrong, make us willing to change;
when we are right, make us easy to live with."
–Rev. Peter Marshall

When Manuel died, I had the chance to speak with many of our mutual high school friends. The response was noteworthy. It was a quiet shock. There were ample sighs and expressions of a deep loss. We all felt close to him. Our respect for him was enormous.

There was simply this huge awareness of having lost someone who had truly mattered. We had lost an individual we knew for sure had lived an authentically good life.

I was not surprised by what I heard, but I was impressed by the consistency of the commentary. Everyone spoke about his humility. Everyone. They acknowledged his kindness, not as some bland empty term, but in Manuel, as a full scope image of someone who treated others with respect and fairness and interest.

They spoke of his quiet leadership and example, and noted he was never arrogant, or rude, or biased. He never called attention to himself, and yet, he managed to bring out the best in the rest of us. We were far more likely to work at being like Manuel, than he would need to work to be like us.

Words, which do not always come easily, flowed with descriptions and comments about Manuel having been exceptionally gracious and generous. Manuel was always interested in everyone, and offered us attention, acknowledgement, and affirmation. He was easy with praise—generous. He refused to make fun of anyone, or judge someone harshly, or even participate in the competitive social climbing of those high school years.

He was wildly popular, but he did not seem to know it. He never walked with a strut, nor did he prowl the halls like a political candidate. I think almost everyone in our class was stunned when he was not nominated to be the King of our Coronation Dance. I suspect his religious beliefs against dancing forced him to secretly withdraw his name from consideration. I sincerely cannot imagine any other reason he would not have been voted king.

To be honest, until right this moment, I never considered it might have been racial, which it may have been, and was certainly more of a possibility than I had ever admitted to myself—then or now.

When my calls were pretty much completed, I thought to myself about how much the book would have to change. I knew he would not want it to be a memoir, or to become too personal. It couldn't lose its legacy focus. Still, I realized I was actually experiencing his legacy through all these phone calls. In death, we always lift up that which we believe to be most worthy of mentioning. This was certainly the case with Manuel.

I was seeing how other people saw Manuel. It was quite moving and very insightful. People called attention not only to the basics. He was smart as hell, a truly gifted athlete, and a fine friend, but he was extraordinary in areas we seldom acknowledge—but should.

He had no pretensions. He was never fake. He was not about image in the slightest. He worked far harder than he would ever admit to dress sharp, but the guy was handsome, had good taste, and he must have known on some level how many girls found him attractive. He would have had to have been comatose not to have noticed.

I think Manuel's religion at that time was so fervently "anti-sex," that this made him hyperconscious of being attracted to someone physically. He would joke about it now and then, but only in private, when it was just the two of us. He never participated in any locker room bragging or lying—they are one and the same.

I think most of his classmates at Horlick saw him as accessible, easy to be around, honest, kind, caring, and above all else, trustworthy. This is no small achievement in high school. To be known as someone you could trust to keep a secret or to show no interest at all in the gossip which haunted the hallways. I am not sure how or why, but Manuel always had too much integrity for such nonsense.

I think many of us, unknowingly, saw him as a person worthy of real honor. He just did not play the popularity games, was not a member of any clique, and paid the same level of respect to kids who were thought to be "nobodies" as he did those who were clearly "the somebodies". We all knew who we were. Manuel either did not know or did not care. He just seemed to float above all that social crap.

He told me often in the months before he died, how he had envied my ease in talking, being social, and working the high school scene—the popularity game. We both knew full well, this was not something of which I was proud, nor do I believe it served me well in becoming the man I hoped to be. It led to compulsive people pleasing and performing. I behaved as if I were on stage round the clock.

## GENUINE HUMILITY

When I was in high school, I dated a bright beautiful girl named Cheryl Kaufman. I truly admired and enjoyed her entire family, especially her father, Dr. Eugene Kaufman. I could talk with him about anything, and better still, I actually listened to what he had to say. I knew he was wise and obviously a most loving and caring father.

When I was around him, I often tried to be like him, and this meant being very calm, compassionate, smart, and a humble man. I think my humility came off as if it was self-abasement, which is not humility at all.

Dr. Kaufman frequently said to me, "Too humble is half proud Bill." I didn't really get it at first, but over time, I knew it was his way of telling me I was working too hard to "sound" humble.

We do not often experience genuine humility. Authentic. Real. It is quite precious and we would probably have a fairly tough time naming even a few people as being truly humble.

Too much expressed modesty or humility is nothing more than a soul on the hunt for compliments and praise. Since we cannot feign humility, it comes off as self-deprecating drivel. Is there anything worse than experiencing someone who is glaringly attractive, trying to pretend to be homely, even ugly? Not only does it not ring true. It rings pathetic.

Real humility is not self-abasement. Real humility is born of honest and rigorous reflection. It is counting blessings, not popularity points. It is claiming talents and failings, gifts and flaws, significance and insignificance. It is having a good opinion of oneself, but also of others. Somebody who is genuinely humble and has a good sense of humor can be the butt of the joke, but can laugh at themselves, and often do.

The high esteem in which Manuel was held, as revealed in all the comments I heard after he died, made me wonder if he had any idea how much he meant to others. Did he realize how deeply he was valued, respected, even cherished? Did he even have an inkling that, above all else, he had been a role model to us, and potentially to those who will follow?

A legacy of genuine humility is no small accomplishment, as our recent political experiences have so graphically proven. Big-headed boring blowhards may get our attention, but will never keep it, because they have nothing to say, unless you like to have someone tell you they are a genius on a regular basis.

Try to put those words into Manuel's mouth, "I am a genius," and you will then understand fully what it means to be genuinely humble.

---

*Real humility is not self-abasement.*
*Real humility is born of honest and rigorous reflection.*
*It is counting blessings, not popularity points.*

---

## SPIRITUAL MODESTY

I believe Manuel retained a deep and powerful spiritual life, but he came to reject the absolute rigidity of his former religion. He still had a prayer life. He still had deep and life-enhancing values and ethics. He took the notion of following Jesus quite seriously. He was not anti-religion, but no longer found it to be healthy, helpful, or even hopeful for him.

Where his religion failed him was in its focus on what **not to do** rather than on **who to be**. It was a religion which did not allow his soul a chance to doubt, question, expand, struggle or mature. It was a religion which sought eternity only in the great beyond and never in the equally great here and now.

I experienced his religion to be extremely judgmental. However, what I now know is that my response to his religion was just as self-righteous and judgmental. Still, I found our debates to be rigorous, informative, clarifying, respectful (for the most part), and a powerful slice of our friendship.

I believe Manuel developed and cultivated a very modest spirituality. His spiritual side was quiet and reflective and was shaped, formed, and fed, primarily by his life at home, with his wife Aurelia, and daughter, Lea. Manuel viewed his spirituality as something private, and in no way, evangelical.

I experienced Manuel's spiritual modesty as rooted in a daily decision to let his actions speak for themselves. He came to be far more gracious in his attitudes and more merciful in his behavior. He truly followed Jesus, but only as the spiritual event and model for Grace. He had no use for those who spoke of Jesus as their best pal, or as a belief they owned or kept in their back pocket, or even in the concept of Jesus as a Lord and Savior.

Manuel came to have little to no use for organized religion. He and I spoke often, of how badly the Church was failing so many good people. We both came to question why the Church insisted on offering answers to questions nobody was asking. We were puzzled by the lack of depth we witnessed in so much Christian thought and behavior. It too often felt childish, done by rote, or offered up as the chant of clones, delivering a supposedly defining creed.

Manuel had some intense concerns about how the Church was failing the Hispanic community. It did not empower or encourage them to speak up and out about the racism they knew every day. Manuel grew increasingly angry at the Church for wanting to save souls rather than create lives of peace and justice and a celebration of equality and diversity.

Manuel often commented positively on the liberation theology to be found, heard, and experienced in South and Central America. He felt, however, that its radical commitment to a more socialist approach to ethics and economics would never translate well in America.

In high school and college, Manuel often told me he was interested in saving my soul. I often told him I did not need or require his help and that I was not sure he had some magic powers to do so. To say the least, our discussions on this subject were intense.

From my biased perspective, Manuel matured in faith and within his spiritual perspective. He came to discern how eternal life was not up for discussion, debate, or judgment. We both believed eternity to be out of the human domain. It was a topic and/or reality which we needed to surrender to being solely a matter for a leap of faith.

We both came to a remarkably similar set of beliefs on this subject: we could not prove the existence of a Heaven; we could not explain or define the experience; we had no idea where it was or is or had been; we had no idea of who gets to go there, or why some folks were condemned to an eternity in Hell; and we intensely questioned the notion of a God who would create a Hell in the first place. It made no sense to us, and certainly inspired no faith.

A major factor in both of our spiritual perspectives was a core conviction that Jesus was **NOT A CAPITALIST.**

The Gospels, preached and taught in his name, are not remotely capitalist. Preaching good news to the poor. The first shall be last, and the last first. If you have two coats, give one of them away. If you wish to get into Heaven, give everything to the poor. You cannot worship money and materialism and God at the same time. Money is the root of all evil.

The whole early Church of Paul was like a kibbutz; everything was shared. This eliminated hunger, homelessness, and provided care for the widow, the sick, or the shattered in spirit.

The idea of the Year of Jubilee, which Jesus, as a good Jew certainly celebrated, called for believers to save diligently over six years, because in the seventh, everything earned was to be given to the poor. In an America which cannot seem even to tolerate a welfare system of public assistance, celebrating a year of Jubilee as a nation is unimaginable.

**Socialism is not some evil system.**

It is a simple economic system focused on human equality. It seeks to regulate and to limit the accumulation and amassing of a fortune. It stresses, as did Jesus, the importance of putting the public <u>before</u> the private.

Manuel and I noted something about Sweden, Norway, Finland, Britain, Canada, and Australia. In those countries, socialism, when and if it is accepted and celebrated, can lead to a reasonably just and fair distribution of wealth, a trust in government (as they are freely <u>elected</u> officials), and a refusal to give large corporations inordinate power.

Many Americans would argue that we can never trust big government, and that socialism would kill the innovative and entrepreneurial spirit. This has been a long and divisive world-wide debate, and this is not the time or place to offer some extensive opinion on the subject.

For me, the bottom line was that a God or Higher Power would never endorse the idea of so few people having the control of such vast sums of money.

For Manuel, the issue was the same as mine, but with a further admonition. A God or Higher Power would never be okay with most of the money being in the hands of white people.

Spiritual modesty is an attitude, a perspective, a way of life, an ethical walk, and a belief in the sacred value and worth of every human being. It is also a rigorous devotion to the belief in the equality and diversity which must be celebrated within the human race.

Spiritual modesty does not claim to have all the answers or to always do the right thing. Spiritual modesty is wise and faithful. It guides the sermons we preach to be delivered with few to no words.

Spiritual modesty does not talk a good line; it lives a good life.

> *A major factor in both of our spiritual perspectives was a core conviction that Jesus was NOT A CAPITALIST.*

## ENOUGH

I believe that within those people who are humble, there is an intimate bond between their humility and their capacity to know when enough is enough. Manuel agreed. We both championed this observation.

Humility regulates the impulse to think we need way more than we actually do. It seems to encourage moderation. It is opposed to excess. It warns us of becoming obsessive or compulsive, and especially admonishes us about being addicted.

Humility is an attitude. It is a perspective. It is also a philosophy and ethic. Humility warns us when we are heading off track. In our American culture, one of the primary ways we get ourselves hopelessly lost, is by thinking we have to have everything we want—or have been influenced to believe we need.

Humility functions both as a yellow light of caution and the flashing red of stop. Humility is on the alert for when we need to tell ourselves, "That is enough!"

Think of humility as having a prophetic function; it gives us insight into the trajectory of our behaviors when they might become gluttonous and unhealthy. I am not just speaking of food here, but our culture's reckless need to possess too much of everything; too many technological gadgets; too many clothes; too many luxuries; too many cars; too much of almost anything you can name that can be owned.

If I walk into a home and immediately see the owners have just about everything imaginable, and that they brag about their enormous closets for storing it all, I sense a lack of humility. They may try to act as though theirs is a modest accumulation. But in their soul, they know, we know, we all know, when we have too much.

I once asked my Confirmation class to go home and write down everything in their own room which qualified as a necessity and everything which was clearly a luxury. One young man wisely said, he would do it if I would do it. I agreed.

It was an unbelievably sobering exercise, and my necessity list was so damn short; the luxuries I owned were embarrassing. It did lead to one of the best discussions I have had with a group of confirmands, but it also made me realize how difficult it is to practice what you preach.

Humility is a way of seeing the world and this means understanding the needs of the whole world's population. It is disgraceful that Americans tend not to care about what is happening anywhere but here. We are often shamefully unaware of the political, social, and economic realities being faced by other nations.

I think humility is an excellent first step in becoming a global citizen. It helps us recognize that our understanding of what constitutes enough must be reflective of our needs **AND** the needs of others.

When I have listened to the numerous young people who are on board with protecting our environment, and support "the green movement," I hear a sincere effort to keep their wants and needs humble. They not only practice moderation, but also seem to understand and accept that they need to make sacrifices.

Humility is political. Humility is economic. Humility is a way of life. It is a lifestyle. When we have a healthy and honest perspective of ourselves, then we will not feel entitled. We will not overindulge or believe in the absurdity of some of us "earning" billions of dollars.

Humility can and does define values. It encourages restraint and equality. It celebrates ethics and makes genuine efforts to grow in sharing and caring every day.

Manuel kept it simple. I never recall him being much of a consumer. He never talked about what he owned. His only delights were in the vehicles which enabled him to still feel mobile. I know he would have loved to travel. But, I suspect this would have been a desire to know more about the world he lived in, and less about making sure he dragged with all the American niceties of home wherever he went.

We both felt strongly that it was dangerous for our youth to be transformed into compulsive consumers, thereby losing their identity, ethics, and soul. And we saw much evidence of such loss. It was discomforting and ominous to hear young people claiming to own so much stuff, having gone so many places, and by such a young age.

Greed and materialism, we both would have contended, are the most significant spiritual issues facing America as a nation and as a people—especially our vulnerable youth.

One last note of observation. When a culture is bombarded daily by the message that it is never enough, it is stunning how pervasive this perspective becomes.

We are not enough as husbands or wives. We are never good enough parents. We are not enough as brothers or sisters. We are not enough as a lover. We are not enough in terms of what we know or what we own. We are never enough in terms of success or power or position.

We all become perpetual adolescents, who are never popular enough, and who simply must have the most recent fad or fetish, as a matter of life or death. "I would die without it," is the beginning of the road to all addictions.

America needs to know when enough is enough. We need to put the notion of "enough" into our personal and family vocabulary. We must be able to say **NO** to ourselves, and to our children, before it proves too late—which is the message of our climate.

Think about it. Take your own personal inventory. Luxury or necessity?

If we are honest about it, it is appalling.

## AN EASY YOKE AND A LIGHT BURDEN

> "Come to me, all you that are weary and are carrying heavy burdens, and I will give you rest. Take my yoke upon you, and learn from me; for I am gentle and humble in heart, and you will find rest for your souls. For my yoke is easy and my burden is light."
> Matthew 11:28-30

Manuel asked me what was my favorite scripture passage? He was truly asking what scripture passage would I like the youth with whom I worked to know by heart. The above passage is the one I told him was most important to me, and then he asked me—why? The following is a paraphrase of what I told him, as well as a summation of his own response to the passage, and why I chose it.

Both responses have much to say about the call to **BEING HUMBLE.**

This passage is brutally honest. Everything is said with sobering honesty. It is at its core—humble.

We are weary, much of the time. We keep trying to win the rat race; but as Lily Tomlin observed, even if we win, we are still rats. Trying to keep everyone happy is exhausting. It is overwhelming trying to juggle twenty balls in the air, while performing all our tasks and responsibilities. It is demoralizing to think we can be perfect.

Most of us have twenty-four chips for our hourly use during the day. The tragic and pathetic reality is that most of us have used those twenty-four chips by noon.

I think many Americans, much of the time, are burned out, burned up, or have been burned down to rubble. We are dead tired. We have no life in us, no excitement or enthusiasm. We slog our way through our days. We endure. We survive. This is not living. This is being weary.

Life is difficult. We keep pretending it is not. This lying eats away at every aspect of our spiritual life, especially our integrity, dignity, and maturity. We all carry big weighty burdens. Major losses. Significant defeats. Substantial failures and flaws. Real hurt and heartache and disappointment. Genuine despair. Nobody escapes tragedy.

Yes, many of us can point to a list of achievements, accomplishments, even great satisfactions during our time here on this good earth. Yet the fact remains, on any given day, our burdens remain considerable. Compassion alone bestows upon us tons of pain to carry.

With all this being said, it is critical to have a safe place to heal, restore, cleanse, and re-create. We need a God or Higher Power who will offer us rest for our hearts, minds, souls, and bodies. We yearn for rest. We deeply desire a chance to get away from everything. We long to sort it out and come back to Life, ready to accept the conditions set by our God or Higher Power.

Shocking in all this, and contained within this profound scriptural passage, are the ideas of an **EASY YOKE AND A LIGHT BURDEN**. Both concepts, I believe, are alluding to Grace.

Grace is unconditional love. Grace is unconditional mercy. Though we live in a culture which expects us to be on the go, climbing up the ladder, doing it all, and being a somebody spectacular, our God or Higher Power only asks us to believe that Grace is true.

All Life is Grace. Every morsel or drop or piece is soaked in the Grace of God. If we truly believe in Grace, then we have no other choice but to **BE** humble. All is gift. Everything is worthy of our gratitude. We have received it all, not earned it. God, or a Higher Power, may offer praise or merit for our efforts, but not decree us to be the owners.

If we are stupid enough to believe all that we have, we have earned, and what we have accomplished, is solely the result of our efforts, then we have no humility in us. None. Nada. Zero.

Just imagine the difference in how we would live our lives every day, if we were to humbly admit and accept our complete dependency on the Grace of God or a Higher Power. We would begin each day knowing we were beloved, cherished, adored, and yes, enough. We would start the day knowing we possessed everything we needed to have a good life. We would understand the role of tragedy and sorrow in our lives but be confident of the balance we would find in the love and joy which is ceaselessly presenting itself to us.

We would embrace the paradox, the mystery, the miracle which is Life, and the Grace which is the ground of our very being.

God's only expectation of us is to receive the day which has been made for us, and to rejoice and be glad in it. This is our Higher Power telling us that in this course or class, we already have an "A"—we just have to show up; be **PRESENT!**

Manuel wanted to know if the people, to whom I preached or taught this theology, were accepting of its wisdom, or resistant. I told him they resisted. They needed to believe they alone could make it happen, offer Life such a full and positive affirmation, and feel themselves to be worthy. We live in a culture dominated daily by the notion **we must earn everything we have.**

I reminded Manuel of a brilliant exchange between Michael Bloomberg and Bernie Sanders, during a primary debate in the 2020 Presidential election. Bernie boldly told Michael he felt it was a moral travesty that he was worth in excess of 65 billion dollars.

Michael defended himself by saying he had worked very hard for his money. Bernie came back with the line, "I think if you check with all the people you employ, they worked pretty hard to get you that wealth as well, but do not have quite so much to show for all their efforts."

There is a bottom line there. Humility would tell us that to have what we have, all of us have been helped mightily by others and our God or Higher Power. It is this humility which will inspire us to help those who have fallen on their faces, to get back up again. It is humility which makes us responsible for the health and well-being of every other human being on the planet.

Manuel was blunt on this subject. He felt that Americans often do not want to hear the Truth. We do not want to think we have burdens, or flaws, or are addicted, or need help, and so we tend to play God all the time.

It is in God-playing that we demolish any initiative to be humble. It is fair for me to say that Manuel exhibited a deep and powerful resistance to this urge to play God. I believe this is one of the reasons he did not do battle with MS, but seemingly befriended it, and chose to humbly do and be as much he could, while carrying on with this significant burden.

Don't get me wrong. He fought like Hell. However, he chose never to see his life in terms of war. He was at peace with his place and condition.

Maybe this is why so many people saw deeply spiritual qualities in Manuel. His were attributes some would have called divine, because he had so clearly and unequivocally rejected any desire to think of himself as being in God's shoes.

Manuel was also quick to point out and repeat that our culture cannot grasp the notion, which he believed in strongly, that we in fact, **OWN NOTHING—IT WAS SIMPLY NEVER OURS IN THE FIRST PLACE.** Manuel saw Life as pure gift.

We both found it frightening and appalling to witness so many politicians and religious leaders speak as if they were channeling God. This lack of humility is seen by people everywhere as synonymous with America and Americans. To the world, these politicians and religious hucksters were in it for the money, and saw others, especially people of color, as their next easy target.

## A LASTING LEGACY

I find it so ironic, even a bit bizarre, to recognize how the legacy we create is so dependent on surrendering, having the wisdom to wave the white flag. In our culture, a white flag is worthy only of shame.

Our achievements and accomplishments don't become our legacy. Rather, it is our character, the attributes which we inspire in others, and our willingness to humbly live by the conditions Life offers us. These are the things that will last and be lifted up.

Surrendering is letting go of control. It is an acceptance of not being in charge. It is an embracing of the truest nature of humility; my significance can only be measured by how I serve and support and sacrifice in the name of others.

I believe Manuel will always be remembered as a good man of great humility, who did his best to share his life, wisdom, and love with others. I also happen to believe this is the true measure of greatness.

The truly great are not about telling us so, but are living quietly and effectively attending to the needs of their family, friends, and the world they live in.

Ask yourself today, if you can name anyone else who will be remembered for their humility and service to others. If you are lucky, you may come up with the names of a few. It is clear to me, especially in writing this manuscript, how crucial it is for our culture to adopt a new standard of greatness.

Greatness is not about our achievements, what we have accumulated, and what we happen to have in the bank. It is always, always all about how we will be remembered.

I think we could learn an important lesson from Manuel in this arena. Humility matters. It is not self-promotion, but it is Life promotion. The great do not need to call attention to themselves. Their satisfaction is in knowing they helped, cared, inspired, and lifted up those in need.

We both felt strongly, there has been a real decline in how America is seen around the world. We felt it was our greatness which was being questioned, and our greatness which was being found suspect. Our so-called greatness seemed to smack of selfishness and a stubborn resistance to share or compromise or consider the needs of the planet, or its people.

It was our deep hope that we might all begin to work to turn that around.

Such a transformation would require a huge dose of spiritual maturity. A willingness to be our brothers' and sisters' keeper, and to share the load. But more than anything, to stop bragging and boasting about being the greatest. Greatness has no need to advertise. Greatness is also never elitist or exclusive.

> "Humility is royalty without a crown."
> –Spencer W. Kimba

# Lesson Six:

# MAKE A DIFFERENCE

"Your life is a message to the world. Make sure it is inspiring."
–Anonymous

"If you desire to make a difference in the world,
you must be different from the world."
–Elaine S. Dalton

"One person can make a difference, and everyone should try."
–John F. Kennedy


Writing this manuscript has been a stunning process. Emotionally very moving. Spiritually quite overwhelming.

I wonder. Had we not decided to write a book together, or chosen the theme of LEGACY, would I have ever truly understood the significance of our friendship in my life? I may have had a glimpse or two, but this book has provided a long-sustained exploration of a friendship which was so very critical to my well-being.

Manuel and I were both big believers in trying to make a difference in Life. We were never interested in fame or fortune. We did, though, yearn to matter in positive and productive ways. Our longings were never about owning stuff or being able to afford to do or be whatever we wished. We were centered on the notion of trying to help others enjoy this Life of ours.

We met in the seventh grade, and I am quite serious, when I say this was our focus even back then. It hasn't changed much, but that focus did have a huge impact on both of our lives. Our friendship was grounded in a desire to make the world a better place. Goodness was at the core of our understanding of any so-called good life.

We were both idealists. We were both spiritual. We both had an inclination that we were being called to something way more than making a living. We wanted to be somebody of substance, to be significant, to matter, and to be important in transformative ways.

We did not have a Jesus complex, but we did believe in climbing up to Higher Ground, and we knew such ground would be saner, simpler, safer, and far more spiritual. Our perspectives were wide and bold, focused on love and mercy.

We both came to have a faith, but one which stepped way outside the box of the religion of our childhood and adolescence. Our faith evolved from noun to verb, from solid to liquid. It was no longer fixed or rigid but moving and growing. We both cultivated a faith which did not make us feel childish or obedient, but one which enabled us to mature, feel deeply, and become real adults.

I think this faith anchored our work with young men and women. We sought to encourage their best. We expected them to be compassionate, kind, thoughtful, gracious, and generous—no matter what. We expected of them what we expected of ourselves. We were not looking to be cloned, but we did wish to influence young people to stand for something. We encouraged them to serve, sacrifice, and even suffer for their ideals, and to do whatever they do with love.

The essential principle of our faith was to make a difference. We were not concerned with getting into Heaven, or being holy, or trying to be perfect in any way. We just wanted to lift spirits, share burdens, and make things a bit easier. We both found Life to be difficult and rugged. We felt everyone needed to be cared about and for, and to be encouraged and affirmed and acknowledged.

This faith of ours was not something we spoke about often, but we practiced our fair share. We had both preached. We had both taught. We both felt fully and deeply committed to the idea of improving the quality of lives on this good earth. We did not care about creeds. We cared about deeds. Faith, to us, just meant shut-up and do it.

Since I was a minister for forty years, I obviously was more focused on faith-based discussions, and the work of enabling folks to find a faith they might actually be able to live with. But both of us tried diligently to stay true to a lifestyle of caring, concern, compassion, change, and maturation. I would expect that Manuel's teaching was extraordinarily competent, and that he knew his stuff, but I also know he offered his students a wise and caring heart and soul as well.

Manuel was not only a great person, educator, husband, father, son, brother, and friend, he was a most worthwhile spiritual mentor to all with whom he shared time. His impact, like his soul, was quiet, positive, patient, persevering, and incredibly kind. We both acquired the wisdom to understand the difference that can be made by little things, not so much what we do, but who we choose to be.

This book has been a real revelation for me. In some senses, a more traditional epiphany, a stunning episode of awareness and insight. Not seeing the light so much, as truly seeing the insides of things; our souls, minds, hearts, loves, the world around us, and the universe outside and inside our lives. This book has taught me so much about what is truly unforgettable; what will last; and that which is worthy of being called a legacy.

I have come to know that Manuel gave me an enormous gift, and I him, without our ever really verbalizing or intentionally claiming or naming it. We gave each other sanctuary. We were a safe place for one another to feel, think, believe, jump for joy, take a leap of faith, and admit to our own huge sorrows and sadness. We swapped despair on many occasions. We were rigorously honest with one another, creating a context of being at peace.

I shared some of the most painful secrets of my life with Manuel, events, subjects, and topics, which had haunted me for years. I did the same for him. Together, we made the decision this book would not be the time or place for exposing or explaining those secrets.

Let me only say, this place, where we could share our true Selves, released enormous energy in us. It was a safe haven where we could put down the façade of, "I'm happy and content and 'together' all the time," created true freedom.

We were always there for one another. No matter what. We could get on the phone and dive right in, as if no time had passed. When we spoke, especially in composing the outlines and themes for this manuscript, it was as if we were still junior high buddies, who stayed overnight and sat up talking most of the night, eating, drinking Coke, farting, laughing, wrestling with how to navigate this crazy, demanding, and already difficult world.

I don't think there was much Manuel did not know about me. I had told him everything. All about my marriages, the deaths of two wives, the suicide attempt of my son, and the raw disappointments of ministry. He wrote me upon the deaths of my father and mother and sister. His messages were personal and profound, and he wrote with such candor and insight into my history. They offered genuine solace.

We knew one another's Racine history, and our educational and professional backgrounds, but never got to know one another's wives or my son and his daughter. Still, we spoke often about the families we had created, and did so with the same honesty and intensity, as we had shared our lives at home in Racine—our hometown.

If I were to say the things I miss most dearly about Manuel, they would be the safety and security of his voice and his soul, how I knew I could truly say anything to him. I would not be judged, critiqued, evaluated, or forced to defend. I could just let it out, let it flow, and know it would be embraced with understanding and Grace. Friendship is a miraculous gift to give anyone!

When Aurelia held the phone up to his ear so I could say goodbye, I heard him whisper, "My friend." That was enough. It always will be.

Manuel and I made a difference in each other's lives, in little things or simply by being present. For us, there were no major heroic events in our friendship, no burning bushes we witnessed together, no monumental achievements or experiences. We created a context conducive to maturation, worthy of trust, and where, within thick high walls of Grace, we never questioned if what was being said or done or felt, would be used in a harmful way.

Making a difference is a choice. It is a daily decision and a devotional action. It is to know we have the capacity to make someone's day, to transform a nasty event into something which reveals the goodness and beauty of the moment.

Making a difference is small, ordinary, and often viewed by the world as insignificant. It is the soul, however, which knows full well, this is good, really good, and Life does not get much better than this. What the world perceives as significant is nothing like what the soul would declare to be of real importance.

I know that Manuel made an enormous difference in my life. In writing this book, I have come to realize, I could not possibly have become the Bill I am, without the unconditional love and support and mercy of Manuel Barrera, Jr. Once I tried to tell him this, but it came out with a goofy analogy. I was the quarterback on Horlick's 1967 football team, and he was the center. I told him nothing could have happened in my football career, if he hadn't gotten me the ball. He told me it was the most pathetic image he had ever heard, and we laughed for a good long time.

Our world likes the big and showy, the expensive and glitzy. It seeks celebrity status and will settle for being known for just being known. Making a difference is being a good friend, or mate, or human being. It is nothing more than seizing any chance we can, to make Life just a little bit better for someone else. It is nothing more than sweeping the path, holding an arm as we cross the street, or letting someone's tears roll down our cheeks.

The following are suggestions for "ways of being" that Manuel and I came to believe not only mattered, but also were being forgotten or destroyed by the inane fixations of our culture.

## WE CAN BE KIND

> So many things I can't control
> So many hurts that happen everyday
> So many heartaches that pierce the soul
> So much pain that won't ever go away
> What can we do
> When there's nothing we can do?
>
> We can be kind
> We can take care of each other
> We can remember that deep down inside
> We all need the same things
> –From the song "We Can Be Kind" by Nancy Lamott

Being kind is elemental. It is the least we can do, but often the most important thing we can choose to be.

It is so basic. It is easy to assume or ignore. Recently, as our cultural disposition seems to have soured, and people have become so nasty, mean-spirited, loud, rude, and cruel, kindness has become something we genuinely miss. It does seem, at least to me, that we were nicer several years back, certainly not as cynical, nor as narcissistic, and definitely less prone to being racist.

What has happened? I doubt there are just one or two things to point to, but selfishness and greed have surely played a big part. Maybe we feel we have somehow been cheated, or we did not get all we deserved. Maybe it has something to do with a growing tendency to find fault with everyone but ourselves.

Kindness always remains a choice. To be kind must be a decision we make, a philosophy we live, or an attitude we have been encouraged to hold. Kindness does not come naturally. It is not a light switch we can turn on and off. Kindness must be taught. Kindness is learned within the family and inspired by adults who know it is vital to our overall well-being—as well as the spiritual state of our nation. Kindness is a habit we must cultivate daily.

If we give up on kindness, we are surrendering to our worst instincts. We are choosing to isolate, hate, live in denial, hide, escape, and give little energy to our relationships. Love is then on the wane. I mean that. We can feel its ebb, and watch it be set adrift, without anyplace to anchor. A culture without kindness is rude, reckless, and extremely dangerous. It is the context for catastrophe.

Manuel's kindness was of legendary status. He simply led with kindness. It was his personality and perspective. I came to witness how hard he worked to be kind. He saw kindness as a practice, skill, talent, gift, and the chief offering of the soul. He made kindness into his second nature, and it served him well in his career, marriage, parenting, and of course, in his friendships and relationships to students and colleagues.

Manuel made his kindness look effortless, but like a ballet dancer, it was the creation of hours of disciplined effort. When Manuel walked into a room, the atmosphere cleared and lightened, and the spirit became more respectful and cooperative. It was pretty darn magical to experience.

Have you ever asked yourself what kind of spiritual impact you have when you walk into a room? It is a tough question, but important to answer and understand about ourselves. This impact will be what is remembered about you and will form the core of your actual legacy.

## WE CAN BE COMPASSIONATE

I would bet, if we were asked to name some genuinely compassionate people in our lives, we could name them quite quickly, but it would be a fairly short list. In some cases, we might feel we did not know somebody well enough to declare them compassionate or may not have experienced their compassion first-hand—having only heard about it from others.

Again, I must say, I believe compassion is on the decline in America.

We certainly are no longer known around the world for being a kind and compassionate nation. This has been replaced by an image of greed, arrogance, superiority. Like Peter Pan, we refuse to grow up. We have grown indifferent and apathetic. Our focus is inward. It tends to be all about me…me…me. We are no longer a nation known for our compassionate focus on **WE**.

We are not alone in this regard, as this is a complaint heard around the world, as we live in times which are frequently cold, callous, harsh, judgmental, and downright cruel.

I am not sure when it was, or why it is, but having a bleeding heart became offensive to many Americans. I would think a bleeding heart is a requirement of anyone possessed of even a modicum of compassion. A bleeding heart is not a symbol for being stupid, being used, or anything goes. It is an attribute of someone whose soul bleeds and bruises easily, cares deeply, and is genuinely concerned. It has convictions about being called to care.

Manuel and I saw a bleeding heart as a blessing. It is a soul which is fully aware and awake and alive. It is someone who celebrates being human, by compassionately caring about other human beings—regardless of race or creed or sexual orientation.

I say this often. I say it because it is an observation which functions like an eyelash in my eye. It makes me wince. It makes me tear up. The tragedy in contemporary America, is how our version of the good life, has nothing whatsoever to do with goodness.

How compassionate are you—on a scale of 1 to 10, with ten being the highest?

Where do you need to improve? How? When? Why?

Why do you withhold your compassion? Has this been healthy for you?

Do you hold grudges? Are you often judgmental?

Compassion requires incessant and consistent evaluation. It is so easy to give up on compassion. Compassion is arduous spiritual work, and it may not produce quick results, or the results may be something we never get to see, hear, or experience.

A life lacking compassion is rigid, cold, uptight, shallow. It is void of tenderness, mercy, and love. Compassion makes us recognize the importance of service, sacrifice, and even suffering—at least to some extent. Compassion is to the soul what passion is to love. Compassion stirs us up, ignites our passion to be of real help and hope, and makes us better people, more inclined to making a positive and productive difference.

Life without compassion is numbing, deadening, and disheartening. Living without compassion leads to sadness, the blues, boredom, depression, and despair. The absence of compassion creates a soul in decline, one which is actively shrinking, failing to mature, and no longer seeking much of substance.

Someone without compassion, is no more than a cardboard cut-out. Maybe a good likeness, but not someone to trust in a crisis. Compassion makes a huge difference in the quality of our lives. It is at the core of our empathy, sensitivity, insight, discernment, and congruence. Compassion allows our outside Self to adequately reflect the truth of our spiritual innards. The absence of empathy is at the root of most evil.

In terms of compassion, I would rank both Manuel and I between a 9 or 10. It is and was a strong suit for each of us, and the result of being raised by parents who loved their neighbors.

## WE CAN BE DEEPER

"I would not trust him. His support will be eight miles wide, and an eighth of an inch thick. When you truly need his support, he will be nowhere to be found. He will have your back, but he carries a knife."

This was great advice I once received from a truly extraordinary friend, Betsy Gibbs. We worked together in coordinating the Shelter Island Community Youth Center. She proved herself to be a leader and an individual of incredible depth and discernment.

I not only listened to Betsy's advice but chose to follow it on more occasions than I can count. She was steadfast and loyal in her support, and in times of conflict, always a staunch ally and advocate. Even if she critiqued me harshly in private, she would never do so in public, and chose instead to quietly lead me down a saner, safer, or smarter path.

She too passed away recently, and once again I registered the loss of someone significant in my life and career. Just as Manuel was critical to my maturing and becoming the man I hoped to be, Betsy was no less vital in launching the dream of the Shelter Island Community Youth Center. Both of these individuals offered a friendship of great depth, and this made all the difference.

Our culture has grown shallow. It is built and based upon the superficial, the fake, the phony, and far too often, on nothing more than an image or illusion. We need to become deeper as individuals.

We need to feel things deeply and have convictions and concerns which root us and ground us. We need to be invested, committed, and willing to be there in times of turmoil or strife. We need to face the real issues, the ones which matter, issues that impact human lives. We need to stay clear of the glittering generalities and inane drivel of the latest gossip.

Depth. Be a person of depth. Offer others a deep friendship. Be someone your children and our youth can emulate, count upon, and trust to follow through. Say what you mean and mean what you say. Be responsible, dependable, do your best, be honest, work hard, be somebody worthy of honoring—this is what our youth are looking for from us, the adult population.

Our young are so deeply disappointed in how shallow most adults prove to be. Even parents, far too often, talk of nothing besides the numbers: what is your class rank; what is your grade point; what are your SAT scores; how does that college rate; and what does the average graduate of this school earn?

It is a shame we have allowed ourselves to become a nation fixated on the shallow and that which offers nothing more than mind-numbing, soul-dumbing entertainment, at the expense of our own maturing. It has ruined our own reputation and been corrosive to the core of our collective soul.

Having great depth means to be a person of impeccable character, someone whose word is solid and dependable, and for whom we can risk great trust and even, sharing our dreams. Depth is missing from the crude and crass and greedy. It is absent from those who are fake, phony, and self-aggrandizing. In stormy times, those trees without deep roots, become no more than tumbleweeds that sail off with the wind.

Manuel was a true and deep friend. I believe he was to many. He was committed to his wife and daughter and tried hard to be a source of strength and support to his parents and siblings. He made a difference. He made Life better, fuller, often easier, and certainly of greater worth and value.

Manuel was rare. He was never about money or fame, or power or recognition. He was deeply committed to helping make the world a saner and safer place. His depth and integrity and dignity were obvious and noteworthy.

I know the following statement will sound judgmental, but it is worth the risk—most of the folks I know, could barely scratch the surface of Manuel's depth. He was one of a kind—by choice, decision, and example.

Be very careful of those whose support is an eighth of an inch deep. If you fall through that ice, you can drown pretty quickly. Friendships of real depth are worthy of being honored, kept, and are never easy to find or create. They are precious. Treat them as such.

## WE CAN CREATE HOPE

If we are genuine in our desire to make hope happen, then we will make a difference. Hope is created not from the outside in, but from the inside—and it flows out to others. Hope is not just being positive.

Hope is not simply being happy. Hope is created by choice. It is a decision on what constitutes our ultimate concerns.

We believe that hope is for everyone, everywhere, and for all time—eternal. Hope is transforming, and unforgettable. Hope lifts us up to higher ground. Hope inspires us to be our very best Selves. Hope seeks to bring Heaven to earth.

We have already addressed some of the building blocks utilized in the construction of hope. The foundation of hope is built out of kindness, compassion, and depth, with words and behaviors intended to make a difference.

It is action centered on **WE**, and not exclusively on **ME**. It is a way of life, a perspective and philosophy, a walk, which is deeply rooted in keeping Life simple, sane, and smart. Hope strives to create contexts in which living and loving and learning can thrive.

In my work with the youth of Shelter Island, and Manuel's teaching efforts with his students at Arizona State University, we focused on enabling the youth we served to believe in themselves—that they had talent, skill, and the innate capacity to make hope happen on this good earth.

We wanted them to thrive, enjoy, create, wonder, dream, risk, and live Life with such enthusiasm and effort, knowing that the difference they made could actually improve someone's day. They might enable the world to become a genuinely more loving and forgiving place to dwell.

We both encouraged our students to learn how to inspire others, serve and sacrifice on their behalf, and indelibly imprint themselves on the memories of others. We challenged them to do the hard work of saving the planet, celebrating diversity and equality, and making tomorrow a promise we can all help to keep.

Down deep, we all know what hope looks like, sounds like, feels like. We even know what changes it will inspire and the transformations it will demand. This is not rocket science. Hope asks us to be loving in our motivations, compassionate in our evaluations, kind in our actions, and deeply committed to making the world safe for survival.

Yes, human genius will create many spectacular and amazing new things in the future, but it is we, we alone, with our collective hearts, minds, and souls, who can make hope happen in this time on this good earth.

One of the major things I struggle with, in terms of having lost Manuel, is how much more hopeful he made me about the future. It was simply by the way he spoke, thought, and behaved. He did not make it seem easy; he just made me know there was only one way to go—the high road, and he seemed to know the way.

## WE CAN BE TRULY GRATEFUL

Gratitude should serve as our attitude, a perspective on our good fortune in Life. When we are grateful, it is nearly impossible to be mean, cruel, depressed, bored, or immature. Gratitude is a real mover and shaker, it inspires us to be our best, and to offer lives which could be called "a living sacrifice."

Gratitude makes an enormous difference, much like a perfect frame and mat for a painting. It makes images pop. It gives perspective, lifts up the light, and enables the shadows to reveal the contrast at the very heart of beauty. Paradox is the soul of beauty and is also how the fusion of lights and darks, and dabs of bold color, harmonize to display the raw beauty of a face or scene or sky or sea.

My gratitude for Manuel remains strong. He was a vital gift. He offered me Grace, insight, wisdom, discernment, and gave my life a deep sense of hope and perspective. He was and is a blessing. Are you? Honestly, are you conscious of the opportunity you have each and every day to be a blessing?

You can be a blessing of Sabbath, offering someone sanctuary, security, stability, safety, serenity, and a time to rest and replenish.

You can be a blessing of Grace, offering someone that vital moment of unconditional love or mercy, which can turn it around for them, or lead them down a road less travelled—a path which leads to peace of mind and heart and soul.

You can be a blessing of Wisdom, offering someone an insight of depth, a chance to discern options and declare dreams. You can help them to receive the spiritual knowledge of what is their true calling in this Life. You can be that gentle push, or even a sharp shove, which puts a soul into motion, and focuses us on being true to oneself and Higher Power.

We are grateful for what is most memorable, even unforgettable. This is why I hear such gratitude in the voices of those I called to let them know Manuel had died. There was usually a sigh, moments of silence, and then an expression of some form of real gratitude. How great is that?

## WE CAN MAKE SOMEONE'S DAY

Have you ever considered what an immense and inordinate power it is, to be able to make someone's day?

It is not only amazing, but it can be miraculous. We can turn darkness into light. We can help someone get unstuck and moving again. We can cleanse someone's dirty soul and leave it clean and shiny, ready to reflect Light. We can inspire love, laughter, and learning. We can ignite hope and maturation. We can heal wounds which go deep and still hurt. We can clear a path, so somebody might have a chance to get somewhere worth going.

We are called to be co-Creators. We are significant enough to be entrusted with human hearts and souls, even bodies, and to have the sacred opportunity to make someone's day. We can enable someone to feel good, satisfied, enough, worthy, loved, cherished, adored, of value, important, unique, one of a kind.

Manuel and I felt making someone's day needed to become our chosen signature style. It should be the way we revealed to the world what were our hopes, dreams, and ultimate concerns. Making someone's day could provide all the difference in the world. It transforms life, by filling in the holes with the holy, and by finding the missing pieces and bringing them home.

The present is our spiritual home. The here and now is where the divine touches the human and the fireworks explode—utter chaos becomes a circular and bold colored whole. The day is all we have. It is also the gift we have to offer someone. Every day. Any time we choose. When we are ready and willing and able to do the hard work of the heart.

How might you make a difference today? For whom? Why? When? How?

What might hold you back? How can you prevent that?

When was the last time someone made your day? What happened? How did it feel?

Remember, making someone's day enables that person to feel beloved; they matter; their lives and stories and dreams and defeats and flaws, they all count for something. Making a difference is simply lifting up the whole to reveal the lovely pattern of the whole.

When viewed as ONE, we can see our real selves more objectively. We are beautiful and bold and true. Like a piece of crystal, seemingly so fragile, but when held to the right light, capable of shedding rainbows all about a room—or even a life.

We both hoped that this book would inspire others to take seriously the opportunity to make a real difference. Making a real difference is to take ourselves just seriously enough, to know we can lift someone up, or share the burdens, or provide the hope to keep going.

We are not meant to play God or guru or know it all. We can, however, be an important presence of attention and affirmation. We can notice. We can remind. We can warn, and we can welcome. We can help others to be somebody, somebody special, unique, one of a kind.

Making a difference is not about enhancing ourselves, it is about enabling another human being to truly thrive.

It is ironic, how so many of the big names in our culture make little difference at all. They are quickly in and out of fashion, and they leave just a trace of legacy, usually just the size of their pocketbook or closet.

Those who make a mark, an indelible imprint, are those folks who literally did give the shirt off their back or offered the helping hand again and again and again, providing spiritual wings for flying.

The difference of making a difference is in the focus—a mirror makes no difference at all but empathy can transform a human heart in a moment.

Make a difference. Every day. Make it what you seek, and do, and see, and live. Be a person who cares enough to create and also cares about what they, in point of fact, create. Make it a choice. Make it an attitude. Make it a perspective. Make it a way of living.

Care more about others than yourself; now, in this culture, that really would be something utterly different.

# Lesson Seven:

# ON EARTH, AS IT IS IN HEAVEN

"Aim at heaven and you will get earth thrown in.
Aim at earth and you get neither."
–C.S. Lewis

"The mind is its own place, and in itself can make
heaven of hell, a hell of heaven."
–John Milton

"Believe in something for another world, but
don't be too set on what it is, and then you won't
start out that life with a disappointment."
–Will Rogers

In our numerous conversations preparing our outline for this manuscript, we often remarked how odd it was that we had spent so much time as adolescents debating the fate of our souls. Trust me, not one of our friends knew of these heated debates. I think, down deep, we knew how ridiculous they were. Here we were arguing about the one topic over which we had not one iota of control.

It was equally strange to recognize how far we had come on our respective spiritual journeys. We had matured. We had grown. Our ideas of Heaven had been utterly transformed. There are times in Life, when our world gets turned upside down, and for Manuel and me, our visions of Heaven were one such happening. We both grew to believe Heaven only existed in the here and now and within the human heart and soul. Neither of us had much use for debating about an afterlife—which was and always will be pure mystery.

We were both weary of the idea of a Great Beyond. And we were angry that American religion is often built upon the notion only a few folks can get in. Manuel and I reflected upon the damage done when one group or other believes itself to be of the select few. Why do we always need to lift ourselves up, by putting someone else down?

Neither of us believed in Hell, in any way, shape, or form. How did the Church ever come to terms with the idea of a good and gracious God, who then condemns millions to eternal damnation in a fiery grave? We found the idea staggering and, well, nutty. We both believed it was far better to create a Heaven on earth, in the here and now, and do so without using the fear of Hell for motivation.

We both had a little faith. Neither of us needed to boast about it or defend it. There was no reason or to explain what helps get us up each morning. Our faith was a verb, not a noun. Our faith was not a creed but a deed. Our faith was a genuine leap. We simply trusted and followed our hearts. We saw faith as a seeking, a way, a journey, a walk, and the taking of a road less traveled. Our faith is something we might point to now and then, like the flight of a bird, or the light of a firefly, but never something we felt any need to capture or control.

In a very real way, our spiritual journeys, in terms of Heaven, became more and more focused, and less and less vast. We came to realize we only had today to work with. If we were blessed with a morsel of Heaven in the midst of the day—we were pleased. We felt strongly that Life was experienced in moments, especially those magical moments when it seemed Heaven had come down to earth. These heavenly moments were glimpses of Grace, and we could only handle them in snippets.

Manuel was fascinated by what I told him about my hundreds of death bed conversations and discussions. No debates—a waste of time at this point; probably at any point. I explained to him, how there were certain concepts, or words, which were consistently used to describe the personal idea of Heaven. No question, many of these visions were heavily laced with religious tradition and thought. What really shocked me, was how the notion of life after death was often expressed in just a word or two or three.

Over and over again I would hear Heaven depicted as a place of great beauty; as the experience of Grace; as a pervasive sense of peace and contentment; and as a vision of love and mercy. Ironically, at the end of Life, people express their faith in just a few words, and when trying to describe an afterlife, they only lift up a flickering candle of an image—one which would soon be blown out; yet may also become unforgettable.

The amazing thing was, this seemed enough. These folks knew Death was knocking on their door, no longer hiding around the corner. Yet they seemed fine with capturing a little understanding of this great mystery. They did, from my perspective, seem to know Life and Death were one, and that, like strands of DNA, were woven in and out of every breath we take.

Manuel and I discussed what we wanted to share about Heaven.

We decided it was simply to encourage others to seek Heaven, only and always in the here and now. Make it happen now. Don't make Heaven or Hell some horrible acid test for believers. We all get Life—with a good bit of Heaven—and some Hell thrown in; it is much like my grandmother's cooking, a little of this and a little of that.

Seeking Heaven in our lives can make a real difference in every aspect of our beings. attitude, perspective, behavior, and lives. Best of all, it will turn our world upside down. The flip side of our world, as we perceive it, is the dream that God, or our Higher Power, has for us. Seeking Heaven in the here and now is transformative. It puts a stop to the futile need to rack up points that buy our way into Heaven.

We understood why the notion of Heaven was created. We certainly felt no anger toward folks who found comfort and solace in picturing their entrance into Heaven as a return to Paradise. Our problem was quite simple and cautionary: Wrongful feelings of superiority could result from comparing ourselves to others as candidates for Heaven. Since we know nothing of Heaven, its inhabitants or how they got there, it is futile to concentrate on gaining entrance to this Great Hereafter. In a quest to feel qualified, some people may mistakenly convince themselves they are morally superior to others. That is a problem.

The Beyond is beyond belief. It is a mystery of great magnitude. It is not up for definition. It is not a riddle to be solved. It is not a theory to be proven. If there is an afterlife, we can claim it only as a leap of faith . . . one of those holy hunches we get . . . or a sacred suspicion it might be so. Still, we will never know in this lifetime. Never.

Manuel and I were advocates for the idea of a universal Heaven. We both felt strongly that, if there is a Heaven, all people would get in free, and if there is a Hell, nobody is there. It is empty. We had no interest in trying to explain or examine Heaven, as we recognized the complete absence of the necessary tools to do so. This matter was best left to the human heart and soul to express, but seldom with words.

What we could offer our readers, was the hope and inspiration of bringing Heaven to earth whenever, wherever, and however we could. We both believed our personal visions of Heaven were meant to be witnessed and known only in the here and now.

Heaven and faith were certainly key topics of many conversations, with the understanding that nobody had the answers. There were no experts and it was pointless to try to convince someone to see it our particular way. We each get a glimpse of Heaven and faith, a few transforming moments, maybe enough to fill a thimble. That is why it is so vital to respect the opinions of others and admit our lack of any authority on the subject; interest, yes, but no defining statements.

## BEHOLD THE BEAUTY

We spent billions of dollars to go to the moon, only to discover the beauty of a blue planet called earth. Was it worth the price? Maybe. However, I would hope we would not need to go back for another photo op. I would think we learned a lesson. Behold the beauty.

Were we to get up each morning and chase beauty around for an hour, the whole day would look different. I suspect we would be more relaxed and focused on making good healthy choices! I am confident in beauty's capacity to offer us a dose of hope, a clarity of purpose, and willingness to receive the day in joy.

While a pastor, I often took groups of youth or adults, even whole families, and often senior citizens, to see the raw beauty of the seasons. I did not want anyone to miss the lime lace of Spring; the bold

Crayola colors of Summer; the flames of Autumn; or the zebra hide of Winter. Each season has so much magic, so many miracles to reveal to us, and each offers a poem or pearl of wisdom.

On one such winter trip, a participant in our van spoke after beholding and marveling at the earth bedecked in thick clinging wet snow. She said, "I am so full, I think I am leaking." This explained the tears streaming down her face.

Beauty creates awe. Awe creates a sense of reverence. Reverence is a perspective of discipline and devotion. This kind of discipline and devotion is required to become an artist in Life, in the living and the loving.

When I have heard folks speak of their thoughts and images of Heaven, they speak as if they were artists. We are artists. We do not need to die to learn that lesson. Beauty offers us the mini-death of taking our breath away, so that we might be awed by knowing we are each an artist in this Life of ours.

If we live as artists, we will keep our notebooks full of each glimpse or glance of Grace our senses experience. We will always be sketching a scene or an idea or a dream we have to make Life even better. An artist always wishes to keep improving, changing, maturing in skill and technique. An artist grows in knowing when, where, and how to behold the beauty.

When Heaven is present, and seeking an audience with us, it only demands we be awake and aware. Heaven is in our midst every day. How sad to be too busy to be bothered to notice. What a waste of a day and a soul; what a squandering of our fortune; what a lousy choice; if we live in such a busy blur, such an emotional fog, such a spiritual smog, we cannot spot the sacred right there in front of us.

## PEACE IN SEARCH OF MAKERS

Far and away, the most consistent and common image I have heard to describe Heaven was to be at peace; rest in peace; they are finally at peace; I hope they have at last found peace. Our imaginings of Heaven, or Life beyond death, are full of imagery, mental visions of peace and harmony and quietude.

Peace is a powerful and transforming image. It helps express the reality that Life is quite often chaotic, confusing, and a puzzle with several missing pieces. Life is not easy. It does not offer us the answers at the back of the Book. We spend a good chunk of our lives being at war with our own souls, our loved ones and friends, and especially those we call stranger or enemy. And let us not forget Life itself, or a Higher Power.

Our earth is presently expressing that it, too, is **not** at peace. Climate change is creating havoc, so our planet speaks to us through wind and fire and hurricanes and record heat. Viruses are bubbling up everywhere. We are running out of resources. The time needed to inspire any true healing for our earthly home is running out.

Two dramatic aspects of being a human being are revealed by the fact that peace is so often mentioned as what might lie beyond. First, it tells us we are often exhausted, and completely drained of energy or excitement or enthusiasm, even hope. It is clear Life can leave us weary and feeling empty, lacking the spark to push on. Secondly, the focus on peace in the beyond, tells us a great deal about the absurdity and craziness of Life in the modern world.

Life today is loaded to the brim with stress. We feel anxiety, fear, worry, and raw despair and despondency. These are the results of living without tangible hope and a lack of the spiritual resources to make hope happen. We long for peace, we yearn for quiet, and we want to get away from it all. The "all" we wish to flee from is, in actuality, modern living—a total Catch-22.

Manuel and I both felt confident our culture desperately needs a transfusion of calm. We need to know contentment and satisfaction; and we need to believe that this too shall pass. The Heaven we seek in the here and now, is the very same Heaven we hope to find in the hereafter, with the perfect peace of acceptance and understanding. Heaven means living in the state of being beloved.

We both came to the same conclusion. Contemporary lifestyles often left humanity bereft, adrift, weary, empty, frazzled, frayed, and overwhelmed. No longer humans laced with holiness; rather, a humanity struggling to plug the holes created by our brutal way of living; all of which was gouging us out to our very core.

Sound dramatic? Think about it. Ask ourselves why our culture is so riddled with addiction, violence, mental illness, and abuses of every conceivable kind. Something has gone wrong, and way wrong. Folks were never meant to see the afterlife as a respite from Life, just as we were never intended to see Heaven as the reward for good behavior or conforming to some religious creed.

Remember. Peace is not an absence. Peace is not the removal of the chaos or conflict or strife which accompanies being alive. Peace is a presence. It is the presence of determination, drive, and a dream. It's the wish to create peace when and where we can, with whom we can, and for as long as we can. Peace is found in the presence of courage. The courage to forgive; to love the enemy; to compromise and build consensus; and to make the effort to learn to live together as brother and sister.

Manuel and I came to a very stark conclusion here. Whatever or wherever Heaven is and however we experience it upon this good earth, in this good time, it will begin and end with peace. Peace is not a numbing void , or spiritual callousness, with no real depth or meaning. Peace is full of hope, faith, and love, and it is willing to sacrifice on behalf of others, and to serve our neighbor whenever and wherever necessary.

It is time we ask ourselves if we are creating peace in our own homes, families, neighborhoods, communities, nation, and world. We cannot throw our hands up in the air, and say, "We give up," and then wait for the sweet hereafter to save the day. We need to sweeten THIS day, here and now. We need to love extravagantly, in the moment, and we must make amends and compromises, and create community whenever and wherever possible.

Give peace a chance. That was a standard slogan during the infamous '60's. It made sense to Manuel and I back then. It did until the day Manuel died and still does for me today. Are we giving peace a chance? How? When? Where? In a culture so bitterly and badly divided, we need to come together and declare a new vision and a new voice—offering peace a chance to mature and grow.

> *Remember. Peace is not an absence. Peace is not the removal of the chaos or conflict or strife which accompanies being alive. Peace is a presence. It is the presence of determination, drive, and a dream.*

## ALL IS GRACE

A wild band of thunderstorms barreled through the East End of Long Island. Trees uprooted. A few roofs ripped off. Streams engorged and flooding. Shards of branches everywhere and loads of gilded, grounded leaves. It was September and this was part of the aftermath of a hurricane downgraded to a tropical depression.

I came around a curve, and from a backroad's slight elevation, I could see out to the ocean. The sky was violently grey and green, and the sunlight appeared as a shroud of some orange melon color. In a spectacular single moment, a double arced rainbow yawned its way across the sky, and shafts of a sunny gold illuminated the entire scene, especially the carpet of yellow leaves.

I pulled over, and took an entire roll of film. It was drop dead gorgeous. It took my breath away. I kept shaking my head and giggling. How did something so wild and wooly, like this savage bucking bronco of a storm, manage to finish its performance with a splendid little miracle?

There are moments in each of our lives, when Life speaks to us, or sends us a message. Savor those moments, and pass them on. Stop, look, and listen. Pay attention. Be conscious and aware and awake, wide awake, and take in all the ways Life is telling us it is perfect and whole. All is Grace, and all is connected. We ourselves are beloved, cherished, and adored. These moments reveal that all of Life is good.

Manuel asked for his ashes to be spread in the Pacific Ocean, near where he often vacationed with his wife and daughter, and where he earned his Ph.D.—at the University of Oregon. He also asked for a portion of his ashes to be tossed into his equally beloved Lake Michigan, which is the eastern shore of Racine—our hometown. These were both sacred soil spaces for him, and in this case, sacred waters as well.

He often spoke of the ocean as where we could see the big picture. The ocean, he believed, was always embracing us with Grace. When it was passive and still and calm; when it was choppy or drifting or whipped with foam; when it was swollen with waves like peaks and battered by winds which clawed and smacked its cheeks; the sea revealed the savage and saintly behavior of something vast and eternal.

The ocean is a whole. Symbolically, it is often holy. When we were kids, Lake Michigan was indeed our ocean.

Our lives sail down brooks and streams and rivers, as they wander and meander and scoot, as well as rapidly tumble and weave and climb and fall, but always knowing, in the end, they will empty into an ocean. Not an ocean which is the absence of Life, but an ocean teeming with Life, majestic and vast in its reach, and one where we never see the other side—maybe because it **is** the other side.

What a perfect spot for Manuel's ashes.

## LOVE LESSONS

There will be no great shock to hear how our images of Heaven are heavily laced with love. We imagine our loved ones being there. We imagine loving hugs and caresses, and touches which heal us whole. We think of this love wiping away all tears. We do not think of it as an elimination of our grief, but as a culmination, the blossoming of the flower first planted in seeds of sorrow and loss.

The centrality and importance of love is a major message of Life in every facet of Creation. Without love, our lives lack meaning, value, substance, significance, and joy. It is a spiritual fact of human life, we humans thrive on love, and when we experience it most fully, we are at our very best. What we see in our present divided and mean-spirited culture, is a people who just do not feel appreciated, valued, and or yes, loved.

Our culture, and we ourselves, need to work harder and more maturely in loving one another. This is not a time for tough love, it is high time we tackle the tough issues of loving those with whom we disagree, or our differences obvious.

What am I saying? I am saying, and I fully know Manuel would concur, we all need to dig deeper, and create a more loving, just, gracious, and generous society. We must find ways to come together, and to overcome our differences. We will never do so if we are not inspired by love.

Here are the basic and simple lessons of love, which Manuel and I hope will be passed on to our children and grandchildren, and even great grandchildren:

LOVE TELLS THE TRUTH.
LOVE BELIEVES IN THE EQUALITY OF ALL.
LOVE BELIEVES IN JUSTICE FOR ALL.
LOVE WILL NOT CONDONE HATE.
LOVE WILL NOT CONDONE VIOLENCE.
LOVE DOES NOT CARRY A GUN.
LOVE FORGIVES AND FORGETS.
LOVE SURRENDERS.
LOVE YEARNS FOR PEACE, AND LONGS FOR HOPE.
LOVE IS AN ACT OF OBEDIENCE AND THE FOLLOWING OF A HIGHER POWER, OR GOD, AS WE UNDERSTAND THEM.

Love does not wish to get even. Love does not measure Life in wins and losses. Love does not keep track of wrong. Love never feels entitled to hate. Love refuses to be racist, or sexist, or homophobic.

Love always seeks to find the way home to a Promised Land, a higher ground, where we can truly live with peace, justice, and equality for all.

Love is not about taking sides. Love is not about rankings. Love is not about defeating someone. Love is not about retribution. Love is better than all that. Love is about the best of who we are, which is why it so often melts our heart, moves us to tears, and gives us a lump in the throat. When God is present, we are nudged to into an awareness that we are being intimately contacted by a Higher Power, and we can feel the love.

There is no love in the notion of white supremacy. The idea is evil. It is based on a lack of empathy, maturity, and integrity. It is built on a foundation of lies and a belief that some folks own God.

Those who feel God is in their hip pocket tend to create God in their own image. In our case, we are witness to a culture which, more and more, paints the image of Jesus as a white American, and a conservative Republican.

God is love. God, or a Higher Power, is gracious and generous. God loves every single soul upon this good earth. We must become global citizens, who celebrate the gifts of every man, woman, or child on the planet. The hallmark of the Creation is clearly diversity, and so it must be for us as a culture and as a people.

Yes, Manuel found the wall being built on America's southern border to be an abomination. He was appalled by hearing brown skinned migrants labeled as a whole—violent, rapists, criminals, and drug runners. The wall speaks volumes, without any love. There is no love in that structure, not a single drop.

If I had chosen not to write this, I would have let Manuel down in the worst possible way, and I now realize, I would have also been letting down everything this great friendship and this great person had meant to me. Wrong is wrong.

## ON EARTH AS IT IS IN HEAVEN

Our earth is clearly declaring we are ONE. Eventually, and hopefully, all the borders and boundaries and divisions, natural or created, will vanish, out of the obvious need for us to become a global community. Every day, in every way, we are being taught how interdependent we are, and how ridiculous it is to have a First World and a Third World, or to have one nation control well over half the world's resources. That is obscene and evil.

I suspect how we imagine Heaven resembles how we think about love. We have a sixth sense that Heaven celebrates equality, diversity, creativity, change, maturation, transformation, justice, peace, and global citizenship. We cannot truly even imagine it—being a global citizen. It is time we do. If we don't do it soon, we will only be imagining smoldering rubble and vast swirling seas.

If we choose to create Heaven on earth, we will have finally decided the public is more critical than the private; we will have chosen to know our choices must be built on consensus; and how we must care deeply about what and how we create. Our world is longing for a new ethic, a simpler and saner way of living. This ethic cannot be governed by greed and self-interest.

The most glaring thing about our images of Heaven is they seldom, if ever, celebrate capitalism, consumerism, or greed. I have never heard anyone describe Heaven, especially from their deathbed, as a gated community, a lavish suburb, an opulent theme park, or a Vegas. What I always have heard, is a description of a beautiful and lovely place, peaceful, productive, creative, and filled with people who are contented and have enough of what they need—real necessities.

I find it fascinating how most folks who express a vision of Heaven do so with images which are modest, humble, civil, and satisfying, as everyone has enough. Everyone! From a poetic standpoint, this image of Heaven is quite poignant and profound. It is equally compelling how folks naturally eliminate greed or private property or luxury from their descriptions.

Heaven, as a poetic vision, speaks clearly of being inclusive, possessed of a spirit of sharing and caring and a lack of hate. It celebrates the truest notion of love, which is to be free of any and all judgement, and rigorous in loving the outcast, the tough to love, and the enemy. Heaven's capacity of love is extravagant beyond belief.

Heaven is an image, a notion, a concept of faith, and a lifelong spiritual yearning. It can lift us up to higher ground. It can indeed bring out the best in us. When Heaven is witnessed to have come down to earth, it reveals the grandeur and greatness within us all. Again, not in terms of achievement or rankings, but simply in the choice to be exactly who we were created to be. When we surrender to the wisdom of our own creation, and believe we are called to be wonderfully alive, then we become capable of building Heaven on earth.

It is the will of God for humans to be human. We, sadly, spend most of our lives trying to be anything but human. We play God by trying to be perfect, perform incessantly, and keep everyone happy. Heaven is for humans, and it is in our midst, in the here and now. We each have the capacity to discern the presence of Heaven.

We have a body of knowledge which tells us when we are experiencing Heaven on earth. Lumps in the throat. Being moved to tears. Having our breath taken away or being blown away. We get shivers up and down our spines, we break out in goosebumps, and we want to yell, "whoopee!" We know Heaven when we come to our senses. We can see it, hear it, touch it, be touched by it, taste it, and even smell it—the aroma of the finest perfume is no match.

I believe Manuel and I still had very different spiritual perspectives and attitudes. Our histories and experiences shaped our belief and faith in different ways. But ... there are certain matters, our ultimate concerns, where we are clones of one another. We both claimed no creeds. There were, however, certain ideas and convictions, experiences and feelings, which matched and were utterly congruent.

I know in my heart and soul, that Manuel would have placed his seal of approval on what follows:

> HEAVEN IS HERE AND NOW, AND IN OUR MIDST.
> HEAVEN IS AVAILABLE TO EVERYONE, EVERYWHERE, AND
> FOR ALL TIME.
> HEAVEN IS ETERNAL,
> BUT ETERNITY IS NOT ENDLESS TIME.
>
> HEAVEN IS THE ABSENCE OF TIME,
> NO CLOCKS OR CALENDARS, BUT SIMPLY
> THOSE MAGICAL MOMENTS
> WHEN WE LOSE TRACK OF TIME.
>
> WE HAVE NO CONTROL OVER HEAVEN.
> WE CAN ONLY SURRENDER TO ITS PRESENCE,
> AND OUR OWN PERSONAL EXPERIENCE OF IT.
>
> WE WILL NEVER KNOW HOW OR
> WHEN OR WHY OTHERS
> EXPERIENCE HEAVEN AS THEY DO.
> HEAVEN IS A MATTER BEST LEFT TO GOD,
> OR OUR HIGHER POWER.

WE WILL NEVER KNOW WHERE HEAVEN IS.
WE WILL NEVER KNOW WHO IS THERE.
WE WILL NEVER KNOW THE WHYS OR WHY NOTS.
THIS IS WHY, EVERYTHING ABOUT HEAVEN
IS A COMPLETE AND LOVELY LEAP OF FAITH.
AT BEST, WE CAN ENJOY THE FLIGHT.

ONE THING FOR SURE.
THE GOD I HAVE EXPERIENCED
WOULD NEVER LEAVE ANYONE OUT.

THE GOD I CLAIM
IS TOO GRACIOUS AND GENEROUS
TO MAKE HEAVEN AN EXCLUSIVE CLUB.

SURRENDER TO THIS GREAT GRACE.
WHEN WE WAVE THE WHITE FLAG, WE BECOME WISE.
WHEN WE ARE WISE, THEN WE UNDERSTAND.

WE ARE ALL BELOVED AND BLESSED.
WE ALL BELONG IN GOD'S LOVING AND
MERCIFUL ARMS.
YES, INDEED, WE ARE ALL GOD'S CHILDREN,
ONE AND ALL.

"Heaven goes by favor. If it went by merit,
you would stay out and your dog would go in."
–Mark Twain

# Lesson Eight:

# CELEBRATE DIVERSITY

"An individual has not started living until he can rise above the narrow confines of his individualistic concerns to the broader concerns of all humanity."
–Martin Luther King, Jr.

"Ultimately, America's answer to the intolerant man is diversity."
–Robert Kennedy

"It is time for parents to teach young people early on that in diversity there is beauty and there is strength."
–Maya Angelou

Imagine. A long-awaited trip to a famous art museum. Your group arrives right on time and buys their tickets for entrance—a little pricey. You enter and begin the stroll about the many rooms and nooks which contain the art.

Suddenly, you recognize, as does the rest of your group, that every single painting is virtually the same. In fact, they are not paintings at all. They are coloring books' pages, all the same exact scene. A sailboat and a sunset, and of course, a sea and sky.

The only difference in the paintings is in the colors, otherwise they are identical, including the fact that none of them are signed. The group wanders for about an hour, seeking some other works of art, but everything is a clone of all the others.

Disappointed. Irritated. Mostly bored. The group waddles out and boards the bus. Nothing is said, as everyone is afraid to admit they hated the art, or at least disliked it intensely; the crazy repetition of the same coloring book page. The bus ride home is quiet, but full of fuming passengers.

You can imagine the same scenario with music at a concert, books in a library, or food at a restaurant. I could go on.

The hallmark of Creation and of Life as a whole, is diversity. When we think "one of a kind", we tend to imagine something quite unique, special, and even unforgettable. When it turns out to mean one after another after another, of the exact same thing, well then, you are talking about major league BOREDOM.

Yes, at times, being or looking or sounding the same, can be comforting, and make us feel like we belong. However, if this becomes our only experience, with no variety or choice, we are left marching in place in quicksand. We quickly feel like we are watching a TV with the horizontal hold not working. Soon . . . it is driving us nuts.

For many folks, diversity is something to be only, if at all, tolerated. Manuel and I believed avidly that diversity was to be celebrated. We thought of diversity as that which offers Life a good strong dose of inclusion, ideas, openness, joy, healing, hope, and feeling alive. Diversity is the fuel which ignites us to take stock of our gifts, talents, skills, abilities, instincts, and intuitions. Diversity is everything that makes us unique—with our own signature style of living.

Manuel liked using the image of a bouquet. He would comment on hating a bunch of carnations, or even being bored by a dozen red roses. What he liked best, were all kinds of wildflowers and weeds gathered together. Now, keep in mind, we did not talk often about flower arrangements, but it was how we found a good image for diversity.

I mentioned that I thought it noteworthy that we are ALL told we are created in the image of God, which meant God reflected every size or shape or color imaginable. One would have thought being created in God's image, meant we all looked pretty much the same—like a son or daughter might.

Instead, God's image is explained best as a vast and intricate and diverse explosion of colors and shapes—like a stunning Amish quilt. Quite simple really, yet also as diverse as the imagination of each quilter.

It is even more amazing to realize that diversity is the one true thing we all have in common. This gives us good reason to celebrate diversity every single day. What a great and gracious gift. No two alike. Human snowflakes. Fingerprints. DNA.

I would think, that for people of faith, who claim and name a God as the Creator of everything, diversity would be celebrated. Diversity, as the creation of God, would be a concept held as precious, essential, even divine.

What is ironic, strange, tragic, is that religious folks create churches or synagogues which are utterly dependent on uniformity. Manuel and I both struggled mightily over the Church's need for polity and protocol and creeds, which stifled the diversity of the congregation.

What was even worse, we held, was how religions tend to harshly judge those who do not hold the same beliefs. This self-righteous arrogance has caused enormous damage in people's lives.

If the religious cannot find a way to embrace and cherish those of difference, how will they mature to the point of celebrating diversity. Religion tends to be rigid, inflexible, and shut tighter than a drum. There is a mandate against questioning and doubting and not knowing, in most religions and religious folk. They may celebrate the notion of One God but fail miserably to rejoice in the different versions and conceptions of such a divinity.

Diversity demands an open mind, an open heart, an open door, and open arms. Diversity asks us to welcome in those who find themselves feeling alienated, unacceptable, and not belonging. Celebrating diversity is the single greatest endorsement of helping others to belonging. It invites us to love the stranger, the outcast, even the enemy. It cannot get much more diverse than that.

Diversity also demands we find and create ways of working together, cooperatively. Find compromise, build consensus, and create networks; and webs which will keep us linked and connected. The bottom line: diversity requires a good deal of work, and certainly is never as easy as being around only those folks with whom you agree— on everything.

Diversity is for the mature. As we mature, we become more and more aware of the diversity of the universe out there, as well as the one inside us. As adults, we begin to fully grasp and understand that, if we are being honest, the two never really become one. Even in marriage, we may become one love, but not one person. As my beloved late wife, Christine, once said, "I refuse to believe that the two shall become one, because we all know which one we'd become!"

Diversity is for people of a deep and spiritual faith. So much of religion keeps us childish, self-centered, and arrogant. Diversity requires us to have the depth of character, to know we do not have all the answers, are not in control or charge, and are not superior to anyone else. It is diversity which demands that we walk humbly with our God.

Jesus chose twelve disciples; in his time, Jewish tradition called for strictly male participation. Even so, his chosen dozen were a diverse group who could not have possibly agreed on much. They came from vastly different traditions and backgrounds, and clearly offered the world their unique and complex perspectives, attitudes, and points of view.

There was Peter, known for denying he even knew Jesus. There was Thomas, the infamous doubter. Judas, the scapegoated betrayer. Each one of the disciples was unique, but they managed to function as a whole—as a true celebration of diversity.

Manuel and I thought the disciples were an excellent example of chosen diversity. Similar to a sequestered jury, the group of twelve was created in a context of difference, conflict, even chaos, so that they could grow spiritually, deepen in maturity, and accomplish more together than they could as individuals.

Sadly, and nonsensically, religions over the centuries have become addicted to conformity of belief, and resistant to changes of any kind. In fact, change is almost seen as being anathema to the movement of the Spirit.

Diversity, not uniformity, is what strengthens a community. Diversity enhances the power of perspective, by allowing us a much wider and fuller view of our world. Diversity enhances maturation and follows the magnificent dance steps of the Spirit. Diversity keeps Life interesting; it calls us to keep on maturing, growing, learning, and loving; especially the tough to love.

## CLIQUES, CLONING, AND CONFORMITY

When we were in middle school and high school, we became incredibly aware of the power of cliques. Adolescence is a time known for battles to be on the "inside" of the most desired group. It was a time Manuel and I remembered fondly, but also knew, we were both in the "in group". We were stunned to remember the names of so many kids who were left out, battered by teasing and mocking, and made to feel utterly worthless.

Truly, discussing the names of so many kids we knew were alienated, lost, and never felt they belonged, was painful. Yes, most of those kids went on to have good solid and productive lives, but we both felt quite certain, they were scarred inside—in the heart and soul.

In one conversation, we discussed twelve individuals, who bore the brunt of wicked attacks on almost a daily basis. We remembered the looks on their faces, and the barrage of names or vile nicknames they were called. They were berated for being too short or tall, the color of their hair, or most often a prominent feature—a nose, ears, feet, pimples, buck teeth, or unfashionable clothing. Those who were neither good students or athletes, were made to feel so low, they needed to have light piped down to them.

We all knew the in crowd, and we all knew the out crowd. We all knew who would attend the parties and dances, and those who would stay home alone or with a solo friend. We knew who would be elected king or queen or President or Vice President, and we knew before the elections were even held.

Adolescence was a viciously competitive time in our lives, and it still is. The competing and comparing wore us down and out. It was an unspoken stress, and today it is the silent cause of much of the pain which leads to teen depression or suicide.

Manuel was quick to point to social media as being the modern equivalent of the Roman Circus, where privileged folks watch the demolition of the unworthy geeks and nerds and outcasts. Manuel also suspected that the immense power of social media made it difficult for the wounds to heal and how easily the teasing or mocking could spread far and wide.

I shared with Manuel, the true deep disappointment I felt when I returned to Racine, Wisconsin, to lead my home church. The church had been led by a set clique for years and all leadership positions were simply a reshuffling among the same names. All decisions were made by this group, and to be honest, even before the Council had a chance to meet—a few had established a fixed agenda, with little encouragement of discussion or debate.

In fairness, many of the folks within this clique had done outstanding work and service for the church, and they deserved ample respect. What happened however, was no new leaders were being lifted up or invited in. The clique became the pastor's "elite inner court". Suffice it to say, there were first-class members, and second-class members, and everyone knew who they were.

Trust me, I made some big mistakes in my first year at this church. The biggest, though, was that I did not pay homage to the control the clique had in defining and determining the ministry. I had lots of new ideas and they had lots of old reasons to tell me why they would not work. I came back to my home church feeling lots of excitement and energy and enthusiasm. I was determined to guide the church in becoming a congregation with a vision and a voice. It would be a place known for service, sacrifice, and a progressive desire to build the Kingdom on this earth.

They wanted the church to be safe, secure, traditional, abundantly Lutheran, and very predictable—these were anxious and volatile times in our world. They believed the Congregants needed a place where they locate to feel calm and centered. Plus, I now know, many were just plain exhausted. This church had long been a center of dynamic energy and with a deep commitment to social justice.

I heard them and chose to leave a few years earlier than planned. I accepted and understood their wishes and needs. What disturbed me was our inability to sit down together as men and women of faith and graciously sort out our differences. Most of the negative comments about me were never said to my face. The ending was not horrid, but more like drinking sour milk– it left a bad taste.

I explained to Manuel that in forty plus years of ministry, and having done several short stint interim ministries, the cloning of similar cliques could be found in most churches. Their presence was an incessant factor in the decline of the church.

When I was Lutheran, and when I became Presbyterian, I noticed folks didn't recognize that young people and young couples and their families were not big on denominations. They were not anti-denomination, but they were looking for a church which inspired them, provided a deep sense of community, and offered a real chance to actively participate in the ministry.

I cannot tell you how often, as a pastor, I have heard someone say to me, "I am not very religious, but I consider myself to be quite spiritual." For a significant length of time, I pretended not to know what was being said, when in truth, I knew exactly what they meant.

People do not wish to have anyone ram their beliefs down their throats. They do not want to conform to the tenets of a creed. They do not wish to see faith as all dogma and doctrine, which leaves some folks on the inside, and most others, on the outside looking in—but no longer with any envy.

They want to belong to a gathering of good folks who seek to find a meaningful way of life, and a point and purpose to their existence. They have legitimate questions to ask. They have doubts to raise. They do not wish to see science as the enemy of faith. They are not attracted to hierarchy, and find the so-called blessings of Heaven, and the curses of Hell, to be more the result of our doing—not of God's judging.

Manuel and I found that most folks who had given up on religion, which included us both to some extent, were striving to find a mature community which could honestly and openly debate and discuss the meaning and worth of being alive. We were not seeking answers. We were not looking to be cloned, or to conform to some set of dictates, like the lines drawn for a coloring book page. We wanted to paint our own Life and faith and celebrate the diversity of each vision.

Manuel and I both arrived at the same conclusion. The reason why we wanted those we loved to celebrate diversity was that dull conformity can be so deadly to the human soul. Deadening, as in having no pulse, little spirit, no capacity to change or grow or be inspired, or to be the one who inspires.

For us, the risk and danger of conformity is evidenced in places like gated communities, country clubs, and gatherings of folks who agree on everything, and cannot tolerate difference. As we watch the destruction of the public schools in America, please be conscious of what an enormous part racism and prejudice plays. The more elitist we become, the more exclusive we behave and think. The less alive we are choosing to be.

A Life which is free of difference, discussion, debate, or the celebration of diversity, is pretty much dead-on-arrival. It is like the flat line on a heart monitor. The blips and peaks and valleys, represent life, and the flatness, well, that has no life to express—it feels flat as well.

## SLAPPING GOD IN THE FACE

When Manuel and I were students at Washington Junior High and at Horlick High School, in Racine, Wisconsin, we were always aware of racial tensions. We had heard about the atrocities of the KKK but had never known anyone who was a member. We were dismayed by Governor George Wallace polling well in a Wisconsin presidential primary and appalled by what little we knew of the John Birch Society.

Manuel told me what a scandal it had been to some of my friends, that my girlfriend, Kim Hostad, and I were attending dances at an all-black club called the COSMO on Racine Street. We were damn good dancers, and we loved "their music." Plus, they were always concocting new dance steps to learn. White kids did a wiggle, a hop, and a jump, and called it a day.

Manuel let me know how hard it was to know that there were many birthday parties, and boy/girl parties, he was not invited to because he was Mexican. He once asked me if I thought it would be okay if he asked Kathy Watts to go to Homecoming. I asked him, "But I thought you couldn't dance in your religion?"

He told me he thought he would dance a couple of the slow ones, which for whatever reason, he saw as being less Devil infested. I told him the opposite was actually true.

What he really wanted to know, was if Kathy would be allowed to go with him. I told him the truth, I really didn't know, but he was thought to be a "good Mexican," so probably yes. He went through the roof.

Manuel seldom cussed, but this time he went off on a rant. He made his point, that it was ridiculous to lump Mexicans into good and bad categories, and who were we white folks to judge. I reminded him that he had asked me. He said he knew, but he hoped I knew how cruel it was to hear.

I didn't know how cruel it was. I do now. I know Manuel hated the prejudice which swarmed about him, and it irritated the hell out of him—all the while having to pretend it was no big deal.

Manuel and I had hundreds of discussions about racism, sexism, homophobia, anti-Semitism, being anti-Muslim, all of which we saw as a slap in the face to God. Clearly, if God was the Creator, then God created the diversity. Who were we to say God was wrong, and we had a better plan?

Over the past decade, we had seen a rampant and overt rise in racism, prejudice, hate groups, and the targeting of smaller and vulnerable groups of individuals. There had been a frightening rise again in white supremacist groups. We both felt such groups tended to believe Jesus was white, American, and Republican. We had created a God in our image, and, as we were told from the start—this is when Hell begins to be constructed.

Manuel and I discussed at length if we could or should include some of our political and social and ethical values in this manuscript. We knew full well how badly divided we were as a nation, and unable to listen to one another or even scorned differing opinions. However, for this chapter on encouraging a legacy of celebrating diversity, it seemed almost absurd to not share some of our most basic perspectives.

There were good reasons behind our desire for there to be a future which celebrated diversity, and we sincerely hope what follows, will be taken in that spirit.

**Manuel made the following points in many of our discussions on this topic.**

Did people think Jesus was racist? Did they see Jesus as anti-Semitic—he was a Jew?!

He made it clear he thought the BLACK LIVES MATTER movement was extraordinarily valid and that all the videos bore witness to how deep the racism goes.

He told me he would have had no problem attending a BROWN LIVES MATTER march, anywhere and anytime.

He found the wall being built on our Southern border, to be the most repugnant political act of his lifetime.

He failed to comprehend why white folks needed to always think themselves superior.

He hoped white parents would truly work hard on celebrating equality and diversity with their children.

**I frequently made the following points.**

If you think being gay is a choice, when did you decide to be straight and why did you turn down your chance to be gay?

What the hell is supposedly on the gay agenda? Give one concrete example you have experienced.

Is America still a melting pot? Are we more like a marble cake where success on the recipe is in not having either side bleed into the other?

Why is it that so many Christian schools have predominantly white students but black and brown athletes?

Is it moral for some folks to make a billion dollars a year? Should the super-rich be allowed to take their friends on a "joy ride" into space—just because they can? Does anyone have any idea of the environmental impact of such travel?

Do we expect there to be peace in this world, as the gap between rich and poor keeps widening?

**We both felt adamantly about a couple of things.**

The planet is in perilous shape, and we are very much responsible.

Greed is the great enemy of our nation and the grand contaminant of its soul.

White folks need to mature and adapt to many coming changes in our world.

Would you truly like living under autocratic or dictatorial rule?

Why are folks swallowing the lie that there was extensive fraud in the election of 2020? Will many never trust an election result again?

Manuel and I had no desire to see this book become a political treatise on our admittedly progressive views. We also had no desire to keep secret what is at the core of our humanity and faith. If we believe in a celebration of diversity and equality, then we must affirm why we will not tolerate hateful, prejudicial, and violent views. We want peace on this earth, but not at any price, and not for only one race or creed.

## CREATING A WORLD SAFE FOR DIVERSITY

> "If we cannot end our differences, at least we can help make the world safe for diversity."
> –John F. Kennedy

I was glad Manuel did not see the disgusting display of the riot/coup in our nation's capital, on January 6th, 2021. He would have been appalled and dismayed. The thought of folks carrying confederate flags through the hallways of the Capitol, and calling for Speaker Pelosi and Vice President Pence to be murdered, was not just wildly offensive—it was evil.

We were told there was love in the air. How ridiculous to compare this riot to a tour of the Capitol. When was the last time five people died during a tour of the Capital? Have we lost our collective minds? Sincerely, why are we swallowing so many bold-faced lies? Have we lost our soul as a nation and as a people? Are we insane?

America is no longer safe for diversity. How tragic and ironic, as we were once the beacon of hope for the concept of diversity. Now, we are so badly divided, we are literally engaged in a cultural war for the soul of America.

If our nation is to be safe for diversity, then we must make some significant and basic changes. We must listen to one another. We must show one another respect. We must learn to compromise when and where we can. We must deepen in compassion. We must care for the truly needy and outcast in our society. We must become a society which not only tolerates diversity but celebrates it.

When America can no longer distinguish between good and evil, we will have truly lost our way. At present, our good life has nothing whatsoever to do with goodness, and our youth are being encouraged often to become famous via evil. Our culture is in dire shape, and I know in my heart, Manuel and I would have held the exact same views on all the above.

You should know that Manuel's good wife, Aurelia, was one of those who volunteered at the wall on Arizona's border. She was one of many women who sought to comfort inconsolable children who had no idea where their parents had gone or why. Can you imagine? Can you offer any explanation which makes any sense of such despicable behavior on our part? Have we considered the emotional damage and spiritual scars these children will carry for the rest of their lives?

Hatred is always deplorable. Racism, which is the hatred of an entire race, is beyond the pale, and qualifies as evil. Evil is the absence of empathy and a complete lack of compassion. Manuel and I believed we were seeing the telltale signs of white supremacy in America and a dramatic call for violence as a primary means for settling our disputes. These are ominous and dangerous warnings.

Desmond Tutu told a small group of us, sharing communion on a Saturday morning, that America was losing the good will of the world and failing to lead morally. He then described what it was like to listen to the mothers of young black men, who had had inner tubes pretzeled around their chests and shoulders and then been lit on fire. Rubber burns slow.

These mothers were addressing the law enforcement and military men of South Africa who had lit those matches and watched young boys scream in agony as they were devoured by flames. Desmond Tutu passed out at these hearings, at the anguish he experienced in hearing heartbroken mothers tell terrible tales of hate.

These mothers were called to speak by the Truth and Reconciliation Commission, formed in 1995, and which Tutu chaired. The purpose of the commission was to promote forgiveness and healing between perpetrators and victims of apartheid.

If Manuel were still alive, he and I would call for such a commission in America. We have all seen enough video footage and witnessed enough racist verbiage and behavior to conclude we need to seek positive and productive ways to begin the hard work of creating reconciliation within America.

At present, it is estimated that one third of our population would prefer rule which is very much akin to apartheid. This is a sad state of affairs and it does not bode well for our future. Remember, this was the same level of support garnered by Hitler before he came into power in Germany.

Somehow, someway, we must start finding ways to heal and reconnect. We need to come together to find a new vision and voice for hope. This needs to happen soon. As it stands, we risk sinking into such a quagmire of despair, anger, hatred, and violence, that we may never get ourselves unstuck.

We are up to our necks in hateful rhetoric, attitudes, and behaviors. We are sinning in thought, word, and deed. Sin is hateful. Sin is evil, especially when it is being done in God's name. Some of the Americans who are being called heroes and patriots today, truly have no right to those powerful and poignant classifications. Those who lead by example with violence and hate, while declaring people of different colors or creeds to be of no value to America, are not offering America anything worthy of our consideration.

The last things on earth we need are more negativity, cynicism, selfishness, self-righteousness, bigotry, or prejudice, and the need to declare superiority, by treating our brothers and sisters as inferiors. Treating our brothers and sisters as inferiors out of a sense of superiority has to stop.

Such behaviors are spiritual dead-ends.

## GLOBAL CITIZENS

> "There's just no place you can go any longer and escape the global problems, so one's thinking must become global."
> –Theodore Roszak

Ramu Damordan is a personal friend. At one time, he was the editor of the UNITED NATIONS magazine. I had invited him to come and preach to our congregation on Shelter Island and he graciously agreed. I knew him to be brilliant, articulate, and keenly aware of the issues facing our world as a whole.

Still, I had no idea what he would be like as a preacher or how receptive my church family would choose to be. He was extraordinary in the pulpit and his message was reviewed glowingly by all who were present.

What might shock you was the fact that his overall theme was the history of the United Nations. Sound pretty dry? Well, as it turned out, and as he was to explain, the actual formation of the United Nations was an amazing idea and journey. The fact that it still stands and functions is as much miracle as anything else.

He told us that the United Nations was purely an American idea, vision, and hope. Its primary author was Woodrow Wilson. The foundational concept was the belief that every nation on earth should have a voice and count as much as any other nation.

It was America who led the battle to celebrate equality and diversity, and to make sure that every nation did have a vote—a say on all matters which came before this august body. America was the champion of true democracy. America was the leader of not only the free world, but of hope for peace on the planet. It was America which encouraged cooperation and compromise and consensus building on all matters, be they economic, social, political, or ethical.

America was seen as a nation which valued every citizen, no matter their race, creed, gender, heritage, or political persuasion. America offered the world the impossible dream of a United Nations, a body devoted to meeting the needs of **all** the world's inhabitants and creating a context conducive to peace and a cooperative effort for addressing the myriad issues of the modern world.

We all know the basics of this lengthy list of global issues: a climate in perilous flux; dwindling resources; mass migration as a result of a lack of water due to the drying up of both water and work; and the need for work; an ongoing population surge; the potential prevalence of pandemics; a growing trend toward addiction, depression, suicide, violence, and abuse; homelessness; hunger; a lack of proper and affordable health care; and an ever-widening gap between the haves and the have nots.

Ramu then shocked us, by telling the truth, by acknowledging that at some point in our recent history, we seemed to have given up on the UN. We no longer felt a great commitment to its ultimate success. Americans suddenly seemed to not care much about democracy; we seemed indifferent to the belief that all nations, no matter how small or seemingly insignificant, be represented equally. Many Americans now wanted and expected all decisions to be pro-American, and had great difficulty respecting those countries which followed a different economic or political agenda than our own. We were turning inward.

Ramu said the situation was now America's way, or the highway. The US regularly threatened to pull the plug—withdraw our support.

As Ramu wrapped up his astute and inspiring sermon, he pointed out the incredibly tough work of caring about the whole world, more than just one nation. He called upon all of us, in faith, to follow our hearts. He believed our hearts would inform us daily how we must love everyone, everywhere, and for all time, as well as forgive everyone, everywhere, for all time.

Ramu made it clear that the sole Law which governed the planet, and its global citizens, was the Grace of God. Each of us was a beloved child of God. Each of us, enough. Each of us cherished and respected and adored by our Higher Power. Each of us deserving to be treated with respect, honor, and genuine civility.

Global citizenship must be built on the **absence** of racism, sexism, ageism, or prejudice, hatred, or violence of any kind. Global citizenship must be established on a firm foundation of being global friends and family, all of us in this together, and all of us dependent on the unity of the whole, as nations and as peoples.

America appeared to be abdicating its principles and beliefs. It was becoming a nation of more and more spoiled brats, worried only about money and Self and power. We are known world-wide as the educated nation which knows little to nothing about nations other than our own. We are somehow choosing to live in a bubble, behind high walls, and with little willingness to negotiate or compromise or sacrifice. We want it our way.

We somehow seem to think we are the new chosen people and America the new Promised Land.

Ramu's sermon brought home an important point to all of us that day. It was simply that the vision of the UN was our "baby" and if we were to give up on it, kick our child out of our home, we would be abandoning the hopes of democracy world-wide. It hit home. It cut deep. It jarred many of us loose.

Celebrating diversity is one long difficult path, and it will require great patience and perseverance, courage and character. A deep devotion to the discipline of keeping the dream before our eyes is needed.

> "We should see the new world order as a building constructed brick by brick and be motivated by the fact that we have only got as far as building the ground floor."
> –Douglas Hurd, *Daily Telegraph* (London)

# Lesson Nine:

# FORGIVE EVERYONE, EVERYTHING

"He who cannot forgive others destroys the
bridge over which he himself must pass."
–George Herbert

"When a deep injury is done us, we never recover until we forgive."
–Alan Paton

"Forgiving and being forgiven are two names for the same thing.
The important thing is that a discord has been resolved."
–C.S. Lewis

"Forgiveness is a gift of high value. Yet its cost is nothing."
–Betty Smith, *A Tree Grows in Brooklyn*

 

    Manuel and I talked often of our concerns for America as a culture and as a people. We spoke with great love about our homeland, and eerily, of the loss of what we had once perceived as its sweetness.

    We spoke of our childhoods, and though heavily draped in nostalgia and sentimentality, it was an honest reflection on feeling safe, secure, and thriving in a sane society. Neither of us felt this way about our own lives at this point.

We sensed such tension, stress, worry, and fear in people. We were legitimately stunned by the level of anger which gave rise to coined phrases like "road rage." We both spoke with dismay at the incredible number of videos revealing bold ugly racist rants. What was happening?

Since Manuel and I were decidedly pro-immigration, and robust advocates for lifting up the poor, we also knew this book would offend many. This came as a shock, as neither one of us ever purposefully worked at being offensive. We had deep values and ethics and we felt obliged to name them and claim them.

One of our conversations centered on how deeply Manuel had experienced the goodness, mercy, and compassion of his students, while simultaneously witnessing our culture mock those sentiments at every turn. Why? When did being compassionate go out of style? Why was it no longer lifted up as a virtue?

I shared Manuel's anxiety and concern as my whole ministry was devoted to working with youth. In recent years I have been perplexed when listening to many extraordinary youth I worked with on Shelter Island, as they lost their capacity to tell interesting and poignant stories. Now they talked only about numbers—the crass language of technology and capitalism.

I experienced a profound drain in their compassion. I also noted an inability to be empathetic. They seemed and sounded colder, more callous, self-centered, and a bit angry and arrogant. I knew in my heart they were the same lovely, optimistic, hopeful young people with whom I had shared great time and intimacy. It saddened me that they were being contoured into a cultural conformity, which meant any efforts at intimacy would be confined to family and a few friends.

Manuel and I had long thought of America as a nation with an enormous heart. We were a beacon of hope, not due to our military power, but due to the might of our belief in the equality of all people, and the great promise of life itself. This had changed, and mightily so.

What has happened to civility? Why are we so eager to demolish and scold our neighbors? What is our terror of diversity? Why do we refuse to embrace a crisis as mammoth as global warming and climate change when denial might cost us the quality of our lives, and we could face a real potential for extinction of the earth and us?

What Manuel and I found most disappointing and dismaying was the incessant bragging, lying, and making things up—storytelling as we go along. How can we be attracted to the pure craziness of conspiracy theories?

We took some comfort in telling ourselves this was approximately only a third of our nation's citizens, but this was small comfort. We recognized what such numbers, when following an evil vision or giving voice to a violent ambition, had done before. Just take a look at Hitler's rise to power in Germany.

At this point, some of our readers might ask what Hitler and WWII have to do with forgiveness, the stated theme of this chapter, and our ninth legacy lesson?

A roommate, classmate, and dear friend from my St. Olaf College days, Mike Peterson (who also just passed), sent me a quote which nudged Manuel and I in this direction. It is a quote by a little-known American army psychologist, Captain G.M. Gilbert, assigned to watch the defendants at the Nuremberg trials:

"In my work with the defendants (at the Nuremberg Trials 1945-1949) I was searching for the nature of evil, and I now think I have come close to defining it. A lack of empathy. It's the one characteristic that connects all the defendants, a genuine incapacity to feel with their fellow men. Evil, I think, is the absence of empathy."

From this point forward, Manuel and I became convinced that the primary catalyst of America's loss of soul, sympathy, compassion, mercy, might very well be related to a genuine absence of empathy. We both felt the accuracy of Gilbert's words, and we shuddered at what they foreshadowed.

If we are becoming such a badly divided nation, taut and tense, and can easily erupt in meaningless violence, a lack of empathy may very well once again be the primary culprit. It may sound simple and benign, but when connected intimately with the evils of the KKK or the Proud Boys, or the many white supremacist organizations sprouting up across our once great land, well, it is it time to stop, look, and listen.

If you have empathy for only one race, well, the potential for evil should be immediately apparent.

As for the confines of this chapter, we would both contend that empathy is critical to the ability to forgive and be forgiven. Empathy fuels the whole process of mercy. The lens of empathy magnifies the need for mercy within this nation, at this time. The deepest longing of the entire human race is empathy.

## LEAD BY EXAMPLE

If you ever had a chance to have a conversation with Manuel, I think you would have been struck by several qualities: he was reserved, warm, charming, quietly charismatic, had a lovely sense of humor, and was effortlessly humble. He oozed an attitude and perspective, which let us know he was fair and kind and loving to all.

If I were to highlight the one quality of Manuel's which stood out most, it would have been his profound empathy. This quality was present even when he was in middle school and high school—times and places where it is seldom found. Manuel was a great listener. He literally seemed to absorb every word you said. His whole being yearned to be understanding, aware, sensitive, and empathetic.

His empathy is what made him such a superb son, brother, friend, husband, father, teacher, and colleague. It is amazing to say this, and I know it might sound corny, but it was impossible not to trust Manuel. He just never gave any cause to think one was being manipulated, misread, or judged. I, myself, always felt heard, understood, known, accepted, and believed in—and yes, also forgiven.

I secretly competed with Manuel throughout all of high school and much of college. He, on the other hand, was simply not competitive. I needed to be right, the best, the most popular, the most needed. He just needed and wanted to be himself. In an age of windbags and buffoons galore, it was so wonderful to have the good fortune of having Manuel as a close and dear friend.

Today's youth are literally begging for adult leadership, guidance, and role models. I would imagine for Manuel's students he was that and more. For anyone who knew him, he was the real deal, authentic, honest, impeccably genuine, and true to his word. In today's America, these are rather rare and remarkable qualities.

Manuel was a truly good man, and this goodness was grounded in human empathy, to crawl inside the heart, mind, and soul, of another human being. I felt Manuel led with his empathy. He offered it immediately and did not wait for it to be earned. He saw his fellow men and women as already being enough. They were worthy of his respect.

I think Manuel had the ability to see others through God's eyes.

He was grateful for them, other people, unless they boldly or cruelly proved him wrong. Manuel saw gratitude as the foundation upon which all love and mercy were built, and he actualized that belief in the way he lived.

## MADE CLEAN

> "Forgiveness is the answer to the child's dream of a miracle by which what was broken is made whole again, what is soiled is again made clean."
> –Dag Hammarskjold, "1956"
> *Markings* (1964)
> Tr. Leif Sjoberg and W.H. Auden

Life is difficult and dirty. It is a "business" which has myriad chances to be hurt, disappointed, betrayed, damaged, or abused. Nobody gets out of life alive, and nobody comes through clean as a whistle.

We get soiled. We make mistakes. Many are whoppers. We exaggerate, manipulate, and lie. We wear masks, pretend, and perform as if all were fine, even when hanging by a single thread. We can ignore and deny, be apathetic and indifferent, smug and complacent—these all yield that deep down grime that is so hard to get rid of; especially the odor.

What I found odd in being a Christian pastor for forty-two years, was how we lifted up Jesus, and all of his varied wisdom on the topic of forgiveness, but we seldom followed his advice or counsel. Most churches are riddled with unresolved conflicts; and grudges of all kinds, are carried for years, decades, and lifetimes. Oddly, most sanctuaries feel soaked in judgment.

I have never thought of the Church as the place to find mercy. I think of it more as the place which *needs* an emergency delivery of mercy—like a thinly insulated home in the midst of a Midwestern blizzard; a Canadian clipper.

Church is meant to be a spiritual family. It is heavy on the family side, but quite lean on the spiritual. This is one area where most Christians talk a good line, but seldom, if ever, walk the walk.

I recall telling Manuel about a spiritual strategy I used at our closing retreats for graduating high school seniors. I would ask them to write down how, when, why, and by whom they had been forgiven, and who they themselves had made a conscious choice to forgive. It was always an amazing event.

The youth were frequently moved to tears, both male and female, by the level of mercy received from family and friends—it was overwhelming. Most youth felt embarrassed and a bit ashamed at recognizing how little effort they had made in the art of forgiveness. They knew they were still drawing stick figures, by uttering an occasional and banal, "I am sorry!" Many also knew they had been damn tough on parents, siblings, and close friends.

It is so true we really do hurt the ones we love most of all.

Manuel's response was gratifying and revealing. He applauded my effort, and then wondered out loud what his own lists might look like. I could sense a quiver in his voice. I sensed a sadness, a weariness in Manuel, and I now believe it was because he knew he was putting the finishing touches on his life. He also knew that a good dusting of forgiveness would complete the task of readying for departure. This is all hunch, but I think I am right.

We all need to recognize how mercy and forgiveness are demanding tasks, and they are vital. We simply do not give them enough attention. We don't take enough time. We don't verbalize and say the words of being genuinely contrite. We fail to take the initiative to do the spiritual repair work, to heal a broken or maimed or cracked heart.

Forgiveness is a miracle, and what is most miraculous, is that the smallest effort, the tiniest movement in mercy's direction, and the results are extraordinary. It is as if we are all quietly waiting and yearning to be forgiven, or to let out the magnificent mercy we have tucked deep down inside our soul.

Can you even imagine the difference in our world, were efforts at forgiveness being made by all of us—as if mercy were our real daily bread?

The healing and hope-filled power of a drop of forgiveness, is like those crazy cleaning products which claim a single drop can do a hundred loads of the dirtiest laundry ever seen. With mercy, a single drop can clean a whole day, a life, a marriage, or sweep away the guilt. It can wipe away the tears, freeing us to enjoy our lives.

## TWICE BLESSED

I think it can be wisely and rightly said that, when we experience forgiveness, we are in the presence of God, or our own Higher Power, and the best of who we can be.

I believe it is true that it is much harder to forgive a good friend, than to forgive someone we call an enemy.

The work and art of mercy is tedious, repetitive, and spiritually exhausting. However, the soul which carries the burden of having been neither forgiven, nor forgiving, is truly stuck. It is paralyzed, and life feels, well, heavier and foggier and sadder.

The failure to forgive is the one cloud which can block out the whole sun, and often does. The darkness can eventually grow into an eclipse.

Shakespeare wrote of mercy:

> The quality of mercy is not strained;
> It droppeth as the gentle rain from heaven
> Upon the place beneath. It is twice blessed –
> It blesseth him that give, and him that takes.
> – *The Merchant of Venice* (1596-97), 4.1.184.

These are simple, wise, comforting, and challenging words. They are significant reminders of why the art of mercy is so crucial to the meaning of our lives.

What Manuel and I struggled with most, in trying to make sense of America's state of heart, mind, and soul, was why mercy appears to be in such short supply. Of course, it is not. We have an infinite and eternal supply. The reason we see so little, is because humanity must choose to give it out, spread it around, or make it happen.

We both felt America was becoming a nasty, cold, callous, and frighteningly selfish place. Of course, not as a whole, but certainly there is a growing trend away from being gentle, kind, or gracious. I doubt anyone, here or abroad, would describe America at present, as becoming warmer, friendlier, or more forgiving.

I felt a safety when I spoke with Manuel, a calm, a sense of being protected and secure. I believe it was his nature to reflect a merciful presence. I don't believe Manuel ever intended to hurt or harm someone, or to bring out or point out their worst. It was his signature style, to embrace you with unconditional love and mercy.

Please, I know Manuel was not a saint. Trust me! However, there were things about his nature, his being, innate things, things which came naturally to him, which are so rare these days. He was a peacemaker. He just did not wish to be battling over what would ultimately prove to be nonsense.

Manuel knew forgiveness was a blessing. He gave it fairly often, and freely. He had a great deal of difficulty receiving it. I never forgave Manuel anything. Honest! I never needed to. When I had a complaint or a point I wished to make, a request for more or less, or some kind of an improvement, I always felt he already knew, and was presently working on it.

Manuel and I, like all of us I suspect, needed to create more mercy in our relationships with family, and within a world at which we were often at odds. We also struggled mightily with sustaining a meaningful or substantial relationship with a Higher Power. The quest for mercy is a long complex war we wage, and for which we often refuse to wave the white flag. We suffer as a result of our own rejection of a twice blessed gift from a God, or Higher Power, who adores us.

We are beloved. It is a shame that we will not claim this condition, as our rejection will shrink mercy and gradually make it conditional. It is like sitting down to a lovingly prepared meal and choosing to eat the salt.

## INEFFABLE JOY

> "The ineffable joy of forgiving and being forgiven forms an ecstasy that might well arouse the envy of the gods."
> –Elbert Hubbard, *The Note Book* (1927)

Manuel loved a story I told him about myself, and he asked me to repeat it to him on a couple of occasions. It was, not ironically, about my getting caught in telling one big lie.

In sixth grade at Roosevelt Elementary School, there was one boy I envied so much, I could literally taste it. He was tall, handsome, smart, athletic, and had hair where nobody else had hair.

One day at recess, this favored boy gathered all the guys together, and showed us a checkered flag. He explained that his father had won a race last night at the Union Grove Dragstrip. I could not believe it. My dad fixed typewriters, and his father won checkered flags by driving a car over 100 mph in a drag race.

I became really sad. My envy bloated. I knew I had no chance in competing with his tantalizing story.

That night at supper, I was pushing my food around my plate, and my mother said, "It is not what you are eating, Billy, it is what is eating you." I hated that she knew things about me, before I knew them.

I was in a foul mood, and so I snipped at her, "Well where is my father tonight, fixing another typewriter?"

"Yes, he is, and he is very good at it. In fact, he is over by the Russo brothers, old friends of his, and fixing their typewriter and adding machine. While he is there, they are going to show him the race car their brother will be driving in the Indianapolis 500. Your father said he would take a polaroid of the car for you to have."

My father came home, and I thanked him profusely for the photo, and asked all about the car and the race and the brother who was to drive. He was stunned by my sudden interest in his work. He did not have much to say, as he said he knew nothing about race cars, and did not understand anything the brothers had tried to explain to him.

The next morning, again at recess, when my nemesis was once again showing off his checkered flag and giving more details about the race his father had won. Something insidious was ignited in me.

It started at my toes, and it crawled up my wobbly legs, over my chubby belly, across my cowardly heart, and out of my mouth. I said to all the guys, "Well, my father is going to be the head of the pit crew for the Russo brothers at the Indianapolis 500!" Everyone was wide-eyed and their were mouths agape, as I passed around my new polaroid of the Russo racing car.

I saw my movie star competitor race inside into the building, and the first thing my teacher said to me, as I crawled through the door, was, "Billy, I did not know your father was to be the Head of the pit crew at the Indianapolis 500. I will be asking Mr. Gregory (our principal) if he can give your father a call of congratulations, and maybe, we might ask him to come in and tell us all about the experience."

I wanted to die. I needed to throw up. I sat down and stared out the window for the rest of the day. I stalled going home, and sat on the teeter totter at Douglas Park, waiting for some older kid to jump onto the other end of the board and raise me up high and get me up in the air, then so I could jump off and so I would crash to the ground—and hurt my rump bad. I deserved it. I needed to be punished for telling such a terrible lie.

When I finally got home, I told my mother I wasn't hungry, and went straight to bed.

She came to my door and asked, "Are you sick Billy, do you need some Pepto Bismol (which I despised), or is there something you would like to talk to me about?" I declined and covered my head with my pillow.

I tossed and turned all night. I could not fall asleep. I tried faking a headache at breakfast, which I had inhaled due to intense overnight hunger, but my mother said I would be going to school. She then reported that Mr. Gregory had called, and I was to report to him as soon as I got to school.

She coyly asked, "What is that all about Billy? Mr. Gregory never calls the house, unless it is something important."

I shrugged my shoulders, sighed loudly, and told her I had no idea. Then I slogged my way to school, where I waited for five minutes to see him Mr. Gregory. It felt like a month.

When I got inside, he asked me to be seated. He folded his arms across his chest and told me a story. Yes, that is right, a story, while I was dying inside.

He told me that when he was a kid, my age in fact, he had envied a girl in his class, and that she once told all of her classmates that she had witnessed an awful accident on a trip up north that summer. She saw the driver slumped over his steering wheel. Her father tried to cover her eyes, but she knew he was dead . . . dead . . . dead.

Mr. Gregory then told me, that at that very moment, after she had finished her dead driver story, he had blurted out that his sister had died that summer. She lived in Iowa, and he said he had gone to Iowa for her funeral and touched her cold dead body.

I found his story pretty engrossing, but then caught on to what he was really trying to tell me.

"You lied too?" I asked. "She wasn't dead?"

"I sure did, Billy, and when my classmates' parents started to call to express condolences to my parents on the loss of their daughter . . . wow . . . was I in trouble."

I looked at him with moist eyes and while suppressing a huge laugh. I told him, "Holy cow, that was even bigger and better than mine!"

Mr. Gregory smiled, and then he said, "Well, not better, but I catch your drift, and Billy, I will take care of everything. I will talk to your teacher. I will call your mother. Your Dad need never know. Now you go outside, it is already recess time. I will take care of everything. And—have fun Billy, just have fun!"

As I was floating out the door, he said one more thing, "This is just between us Billy. This is not the kind of story we want to get around." I nodded fiercely in agreement.

"But Mrs. Huff said she was going to ask my Dad to come in to give a talk on the race, and, I sure don't . . ."

"Billy, I will take care of it. I will simply explain to Mrs. Huff that you meant no harm, and I will make sure no invitation is extended."

When I closed his door and flew outside, I was soaring on the wings of mercy. I was so joyful, I raced all around the playground, saying nice things to my classmates, and even asking my sworn enemy if I could take one more look at his checkered flag.

I think Manuel loved the story, because it was so honest and real and tender and heartbreaking. Being caught in a lie, yikes, a child's worst nightmare.

Living a lie before God, or our Higher Power, is an adult's worst nightmare.

The joy of mercy is something to behold. Think about this reality—we have such a transforming gift to offer to others, and we can receive the same gift from our Higher Power. It is ready and waiting and available. It is an ongoing presence in our lives.

Manuel made an important comment about this story. He told me he felt it was sad we failed to celebrate the transforming power of mercy more often. He said that there were so many times, when just applying a little mercy, would have made all the difference in the world. Too true.

Mainly, he loved the story, because he knew I was prone to exaggeration, and it gave him a chance to enjoy the glee of seeing me get caught.

## EVERYONE...EVERYWHERE...ETERNALLY

Mercy and forgiveness are composed of glances and glimpses of Grace. It is best that we keep nudging our souls in the direction of forgiving. The closer we get, the more likely we are to forget the event or experience which made us feel so wounded. Once forgotten, it will be officially forgiven.

I think it wise, as did Manuel, to recognize the need to treat mercy and forgiveness as a whole. We must work to be forgiving of everyone, everywhere, and eternally. We either believe Grace to be true, or we don't. We either receive the embrace of Grace, or we reject it. We either offer said Grace to our lives and Selves and world, as well as our God or Higher Power, or it will ultimately be squandered and wasted.

For Manuel and I, Grace was true. We believed in it. We were convinced it had real healing powers and potential. We knew it must be given and received without any conditions at all.

We also knew that together mercy and forgiveness were a process.

At times, a long and difficult journey. It is a journey made in steps, not strides. It is a pilgrimage which requires patience, perseverance, and a true drive to deliver the goods—the divine sanction of being fully forgiven.

Just think of the last time you were genuinely forgiven. Did it not feel exquisite, like a fresh start, a state of newness, a chance to be your best Self again? When being forgiven, we seldom examine the motivation of the forgiver, or even the integrity of the mercy itself. We simply rejoice at the peace it restores in our souls and lives.

This is wise. We could endlessly speculate about the purity of the mercy, or the love of the forgiveness. But neither, like faith itself, neither can be proven or explained or even defended. They can only and always be received.

Forgiving, or being merciful, is the closest we will ever come to being truly created in the image of God.

> "Until you can leave the matter of forgiveness to God,
> you will not have acquired humility."
> –Colleen McCullough

# Lesson Ten:

# A LEGACY IS ETERNAL

"Snatching the eternal out of the desperately fleeting
is the great magic trick of human existence."
–Tennessee Williams, *New York Times*

Many of us think of eternity as just a matter of time. Many others think of it as endless time. I think of eternity as the absence of time.

When time goes missing, or we lose track of it, we are usually doing or being something quite special, something which makes us feel whole—wonderful, even a bit giddy.

When time disappears, it has been transformed. What it becomes is magical; a mystery, maybe even a miracle. A vanished moment of time floats above, about, and within us, expanded with meaning, value, and worth.

When time takes a hike, it often takes us with it—to share in the adventure. Where we go nobody knows and we were never meant to know. Knowing where we are going is simply beyond belief. We have to trust our hearts and follow. Our path must lead somewhere and all the signs point to somewhere good.

When we enter eternity, though we will not know where we are geographically, we will know where we are at—from a spiritual perspective. We will know we have located a Heaven come to earth. We will have gained access to a piece of Paradise. We will have arrived at a place of peace, which does pass all understanding. It feels centered and still.

Eternity is full of those moments which are truly unforgettable. Eternity never shrinks. It is always expanding, but not in the sense of physical growing, but rather more in maturing. It deepens, broadens, and widens our love and mercy. It is the Spirit doing stretching exercises.

In our day to day lives, we incessantly tell ourselves we do not have the time to love more, or sacrifice more, or serve more, or be more willing to show mercy. When we enter eternity, it is not that we think we can do it all, but we have greater energy and enthusiasm to do and be what matters.

This point is called the now. It is the absolute and utter present. C.S. Lewis wisely observed that the present is the very point at which time touches eternity. Only at those times, when we are living fully and honestly in the now, are we experiencing a dimension we call eternity.

I like that thought. I like it a lot. It is like being the PEANUTS character, Pigpen, only it is not dust and dirt swirling above our heads, but the wind we have managed to catch—the eternal winds of Heaven.

A legacy is eternal. A legacy is also what we leave behind which is unforgettable and which has made a world of difference. A legacy is what we contribute in the name of love and mercy, service and sacrifice—all our legitimate attempts to make the world a better place for everyone.

A legacy is not about collecting money or gathering stuff. A legacy is a quality of Life and the enduring offering of our own souls. I would contend that a legacy is largely composed of kindness, generosity, graciousness, forgiveness. It represents choices made when we are being people of great integrity, dignity, and maturity.

A legacy is a poem about what matters in our lives—not a memoir, which chronicles our accomplishments and achievements. A legacy offers concepts which are simple and straightforward, and yet, manage to capture the mysterious love and mercy we each have received and given.

Whenever I give a funeral eulogy or homily, I strive to lift up the legacy left by the person departed. Why? It's important for everyone and exactly what I wish to do at this point. I wish to share with you the three major components of Manuel's life, from my perspective.

Since the day he died, I have wondered what I would have said at his funeral, and now I will indulge myself by doing so. I know Manuel would not have wanted me to share such a focus on him, but then again, he didn't lose me, I lost him.

I need to share what I saw, felt, experienced, knew, and believed about Dr. Manuel Barrera Jr., because he mattered. Even after death, he can teach us a good deal about the meaning of actualizing GREATNESS in our own lives. His modesty and humility were the elements in the soil where the seeds of his greatness were sown. His core, soul, or heart, or whatever we might call it, was pure and fiercely committed to life and love and mercy.

I pay tribute to him, not to worship or adore him, but to pass on to the reader a sense of who he was to me. But more importantly, I want to explain the essence of the man he became for us all. He was not perfect. He was no saint. However, his goodness was exceptional. He truly accomplished great things by keeping himself in superb focus, and on some level of his being, always knowing—by maintaining an awareness of—where he was going.

The goal of this manuscript was to offer our readers what we both had learned from Life, and what lessons we would hope to pass on. Manuel's life is worthy of review and reflection, as most of those who got to know him, even slightly, felt there was something truly great about him.

I am one of those folks—I knew a man who I cherished as a friend and deeply admired as a husband, father, brother, and teacher. He educated us on what matters in life and what gives it a purpose and a point. He taught a master's class on greatness. For Manuel, greatness was about goodness and Grace, never about celebrity or spotlights.

## MANUEL WAS MATURE

"Memories are the key not to the past, but to the future."
–Corrie Ten Boom, *The Hiding Place*

I think many people would have called Manuel an old soul, long before he got old, or slightly old, as we both described it.

Even in middle school, when Manuel and I were notorious for long lakefront walks and talks, there was something about him. He wasn't just smart, though his brilliance was truly evident even then, but he seemed to think a lot, and do so seriously, contemplatively, reflecting on everything from politics to poetry to, of course, all the God stuff.

He was normal. He talked about the then Milwaukee Braves, the Green Bay Packers, Horlick's Coach Fishbain, and very occasionally—about select girls. But he did not gossip. He was never mean or nasty, rather, always sensitive and insightful. He had a positive take on most everything, but would hint at topics he struggled with—secrets, family flaws, and the gnat-like nuisance worries and anxieties of adolescence.

It was a little weird. Odd. I so clearly recall knowing Manuel was, well, shy, somewhat insecure, socially awkward, and quite reluctant to just let go or lose control. He never lost control, at least not that I ever witnessed. But . . . it seemed something quite pure and steely strong abided in his core. He was rock solid.

He was on a mission. He was going someplace. He needed to get things done. I never knew then what this was all about and I doubt he did either. But I do now. I could write a book about it. So, I am.

I think this core was his soul and he took better care of his soul than most guys our age—we both did. He had great drive, and he was determined to make a mark, a difference, have a positive impact on his world.

Now, I would simply say Manuel was quite mature at a very young age. I believe genuine maturity is about the capacity to cope effectively; to be responsible for our actions; face consequences; be a most dependable friend; and to feel somehow "called" to do and be someone special.

Maturity is knowing we are quite insignificant in the scheme of things, while simultaneously understanding how important it is for us to be dynamically creative and skilled. We must offer our gifts up to life itself. This is our offering. This is our significance.

Manuel was mature, a real adult you could count on, and an individual with great character and integrity. Manuel was not after the spotlight, interested in being known for being known, or any of the celebrity-styled silliness. Instead, he wanted to be of help and hope.

His maturity was evidenced by how much he helped others. His help was incessant, ceaseless, and consistent. If you needed Manuel, he was there. He did wait for you to ask, but when you did, he responded quickly and effectively.

Enough said. Manuel was indeed mature. His was not the bragging and boasting and self-righteous brand of maturity of so many men in our culture today. No. Manuel's was a deeper, fuller, and finer type of maturity which revealed a greatness rooted in raw and real humility. If only we would each strive for his level of maturity!

As we age, I believe we become more attracted to those who choose their words carefully, appreciate silence, and let their actions speak for them. I will candidly tell you this is where I was often Manuel's opposite. I was and am a talker and a dreamer. I dreamed out loud, and I dreamed big. Still, Manuel did trust me. He trusted my love and insight and even my words.

No matter what, I can admit that I envied his simple elegant graciousness—he was an old-fashioned gentleman, in the best sense of the term. He envied me my charisma and capacity to spin a yarn or speak spontaneously on a wide range of topics. We were one another's fans.

As I age, I know in my heart that Manuel's greatness will stand the test of time, far better than my charisma and charm shall. However, I am wise enough to follow his example, and I believe I am maturing in every facet of my life: as an individual, a father, a grandfather, a citizen, and most of all, as a human being.

I can also acknowledge that losing him has inspired some maturity work on my part, and on his behalf. I have to choose to mature. I really do. Manuel matured as if it were second nature. Maturity came naturally to him—I think it always did.

## MANUEL WAS FOCUSED

> "Let me tell you the secret that has led me to my goal.
> My strength lies solely in my tenacity."
> –Louis Pasteur

I believe the key ingredient in maturity is to pay attention. We must take notice of what is going on inside and outside ourselves. Our focus needs to be far more about WE and far less about ME, ME, ME. Our culture has become tragically fixated on the individual and the ego. We have lost sight of our neighbor physically, emotionally, and even spiritually.

Here again, Manuel was quite mature. Manuel's eyes, heart, mind, and door were always wide open. His focus was on his wife and daughter, his family, and his students. He also had a remarkable awareness of the world around him, and the issues we face as a nation.

Manuel had the maturity to know the deep roots of racism in this country. He understood we were a nation which tended to pay homage to white folks and that whites had a built-in advantage most of the time. He was also conscious how pathetic it was, how so many white folks in America begrudge people of color having any efforts made on their behalf.

Much of white America believes we share an even playing field. Well, this white male knows the playing field is not even close to being even or fair. Manuel was grateful I shared his views on this matter.

Manuel was knowledgeable on a wide range of issues facing our culture: climate control; the myriad wildfires; the vast complexities of migration; the neglect of mental health guidance and leadership; gun control and violence; the dwindling of our resources and water supply; a lack of focus on public education, public health, public transportation, and public assistance. Manuel paid close attention to the spiritual condition of our nation.

I would say Manuel was fiercely and maturely focused on a few issues, some of which have already been acknowledged here. By way of review, might I say that Manuel was rigorous in addressing the issues facing Hispanics in America; in the ongoing battle to end racism in our nation; and in the need to expand our effort in all things public, especially education and health care, including mental health. These were the issues he spoke to me about most often, and with the greatest intensity.

Manuel's focus was wisely on utilizing today to prepare for making an even better tomorrow.

## MANUEL WAS GRACIOUS

"Ask any person what he thinks matters most in human conduct: five to one his answer will be 'kindness.'"
–Kenneth Clark

When I was a kid, I thought Grace was what we said at dinner on Christmas Eve and Easter, and when we ate at Grandma's, or at a Catholic home; and a smattering of really devout Lutherans. It was the way we said thanks to God for the good eats.

Well, that **is** part of it.

As I aged, I thought it meant God is love and God loves us all.

Well, that was also part of it—a bigger part.

In Seminary, we were taught that Grace is the unconditional love and mercy of God. I tried hard to think about loving someone, anyone really, without conditions, and it seemed almost impossible. I thought about forgiving someone without conditions, and that seemed even more impossible, if there is such a thing, as more impossible.

Since impossible is God's forte—it kind of made sense.

So, it fit, and became a huge part of my understanding of Grace—the Grace of God.

Then I got married and raised a child and ministered to a congregation, and I spent a lot of time trying to sneak in a few conditions along the way. I like being affirmed. I need to be thanked. I felt I had earned a break now and then, and I meant "break" in every sense of the word.

This too became a sizeable piece of my thoughts about Grace.

Then I lost two wives, and a great many friends, and Grace became how I knew I needed to love unconditionally, and forgive unconditionally, and to try and do so every single day.

I got it. The whole package. But it was one big load to carry. Such a burden, and a major obstacle to having a great day for myself.

Following Jesus is like the Jews following Moses in the desert—forty years . . . and we still don't know where we are going; I think I have a better idea!

It gets tough to follow a leader who keeps asking the impossible.

When I was a little kid, my grandmother always told me, "With God, all things are possible!" Damn. This thought had me coming and going.

I envied Manuel his graciousness. I really did. It has never been a habit for me, or a propensity, but always a laborious chore and difficult decision.

It is not easy, but I try, and I mean—I try hard.

## ONE OF THE GREATS

"Greatness is not found in possessions, power, position, or prestige. It is discovered in goodness, humility, service, and character."
–William Arthur Ward

Manuel was considered by many, if not by most, to be a truly lovely and great guy. In all the discussions I had following his death, not a single negative comment was made, not a one. What I heard was how unique Manuel was. Yet what they were calling attention to was simply his goodness, kindness, and capacity to work on behalf of the betterment of our world, and to bring out the very best in us all.

In my mind, he qualifies as one of the truly great. He never needed to tell you he was a genius or the only one who knew how to get it done. He never lied or boasted or blamed. He was sincere and sweet, and yet, remarkably strong. He was rare. He would have said that he was not rare, but our culture often ignored guys like him. Maybe he was right.

This I know for sure. I have never met anyone finer. I have never trusted anyone so completely. I have never admired anyone more. A feeling of having been amply blessed by his friendship, remains in my heart and fills my soul.

Though later in life, we both chose to avoid most things branded as religious, I can still say this from the heart—Manuel was as close to how I imagine Jesus, as anyone I have ever known. I am not talking about the Church inspired hoopla which mandated Jesus be known as Lord and Savior, but simply and solely, Jesus the man. Jesus as just a man, was and is more than enough for me, and for my faith; just as Manuel, was more than enough as a friend, role model, and confidant.

Funny word—JUST. Like just human. Sounds so small but covers such a vast territory. Much of what we refer to as JUST, just happens to be eternal as well.

Well, I am coming to the point of wrapping things up, and I am having two startlingly different feelings or experiences.

First, there is a sweet sadness. It has been great fun to try to document the intimate core of a friendship of sixty years and to offer up our extensive conversations on legacy.

It has been tougher than I ever expected, as I could not bounce ideas and thoughts off of Manuel's gifted and talented brain. I did my best. He knows that and so do I. I expect you—the readers—do as well.

The sweetness is in knowing we tried to leave something of quality behind. What gave our lives meaning, purpose, and hope; our legacies, what we found unforgettable, and needed to share with others. He would be proud of the effort. It is the gift of a friendship, and it was a blessing to have it culminate in this manuscript.

Second, there is the keen awareness of how much I never knew about Manuel. His entire adulthood. His marriage. His parenting. I did not know Aurelia. I did not know Lea. I never saw him teach. I never met his students or colleagues. All of this, I have garnered from what I knew of him from our days in Racine, and from calls and correspondence which spanned the years.

It is like an iceberg. We know we are only seeing the tip, but below the surface, is the bulk of the berg. We know it is there, but we cannot see it. This mammoth missing piece is present on these pages, and every word I have written knows full well how little I actually know.

However, I truly believe all the stories, sayings, parables, myths, and poems of Manuel's life will go on being told, and listened to, and I think what I have highlighted will show up again in other people's words and descriptions of a great man's good life.

I know his humility will be mentioned with quiet dignity, and it will be given the full respect this quality of character so justly deserves.

Manuel's legacy is solid, secure, and inspiring. It has been a gift to me, and now, to you as well. He never sought recognition, but he would be pleased to know he left so much that mattered to us all. He left such simple gifts of goodness. He lifted up ultimate concerns of rich and deep value, which inspired many others to be their very best Selves.

"Well done, good and faithful servant!"—I said that often in my ministry but applied it to very few lives; Manuel being one; one of a kind.

# POSTSCRIPT

What has barely been touched upon in these pages, is how Manuel coped with MS for forty years. This is because I never experienced it directly. When I would ask him how he was feeling, he would always say, "Never felt better!" This was simply how he was and how he chose to cope.

I know that it was often a grueling and disheartening journey. I know it was terribly difficult to never know where the disease was headed or how the day might be impacted. I know he did his best. I know it was Aurelia and Lea who knew the true effect of the disease upon Manuel's life.

I am left with the image of a man who carried his burden with great maturity, dignity, and integrity. Even when we spoke at Christmas, just before he was to die from MS, he addressed the topic of his illness like a visiting relative he had to put up with.

I think he died as he lived, with great humility, a healthy mix of anxiety and calm, and a quiet knowledge that the end was near. I believe it was Aurelia and Lea who helped free him to let go. I know others helped make his passing easier on him, but it was his wife and daughter who gently eased him to the other side.

Aurelia made sure I had a chance to say goodbye. I will always be grateful for that gift. I will never forget the emptiness which hung in the air, right after I hung up. It was like a thick wet towel being placed over my head. It felt so heavy.

There are losses which never fade, in fact, they may actually become brighter and sharper over time, in much better focus. As the months pass, I not only miss Manuel, but more importantly, I recognize far more his profound impact on my life.

We each have very few friends with whom we share the "all" of life, and where our trust and respect are full and authentic. These friendships are not only unforgettable, they bring significant transformation to our days.

I have a wish now, which I did not have until the day I completed this manuscript. I wish I had gotten the chance to have a "journey" with Manuel, a bit of travel, a time to wander and wonder and joke and reminisce, and just think about what mattered in our lives.

This book is now here, and it is real, but I often fantasize about having had the chance to experience the pages of this book, in real time spent with a good old friend.

I guess, I still wish I had had some time with him before he died. Nothing more. Nothing less. We cared about each other at a distance for a lot of years. I guess, when we suffer a loss, one which hurts and makes us wince, we yearn to have had just one more day. A good day. A day spent being and doing whatever we wished.

My remembrance time of Manuel is filled with fantasies of what such a day might have been like. Funny, but I doubt it would be spent trying to do something unique or spectacular. I would imagine it to be a great one, like our high school days, when it was more than enough to just hangout.

I know we would drive all over Racine again. We would haunt our old neighborhoods and schools and favorite restaurants. We could never get enough of knowing it was still there, enshrouding our blessed memories of childhood.

Yes, I am very happy I made the decision to write this book. I know it would have been a finer and deeper and fuller book had Manuel lived. Still, it has been well worth the effort.

Life. So brief and vast and full and sparce, and such a wild ride. I experienced so much. I barely scratched the surface. The mysteries win in the end. The miracles were plentiful. The magic was incessant.

There are no words. There are these words. There are more stories to be told.

I shared a lot of life with Manuel. I hope this helps you better understand our friendship, our shared perspectives, and the power of faith and hope and love, which only a truly good friend can offer, know, and experience.

Manuel was a blessing in my life. I suspect he may have been a blessing in yours. For this crazy culture of ours, his memory, his legacy, his bright light, offers us a hope filled blessing for the days ahead.

Manuel, I will pray every day, and do what I can where I can, to knock down that damn abominable wall.

I am sorry for for all the BS and nonsense and cruelty you endured from white folks who mistakenly thought they were better, smarter, wiser. I will continue to work daily, to mentor white folks in the celebration of diversity, and to disown their frequent notion that God is white.

# ACKNOWLEDGEMENTS

I wish to thank Manuel's entire family, for their generous and gracious support of this book, and for sharing Life with me for a good many years. You were and are a good family. Manuel felt that deeply.

To Aurelia and Lea Barrera, for enabling me to get this book published, and for being the heart and soul of Manuel's life.

To all of the members of Aurelia's beloved family, as well as all of the Arizona State colleagues and students who knew Manuel, I have heard so much about you over the years, and you were indeed cherished and adored.

To Linda Bolles, for your steadfast friendship, and being exactly who your brother told me you would be—I am so glad I followed his advise.

To Nancy Neider, for improving the manuscript tremendously, and getting it in such good shape for submission. Your friendship has been a real blessing.

To Faye Becker, for being a champion of the project, and an extraordinary woman of great beauty inside and out. Renewing our friendship has been a gift.

To Gary Lequia and Bob Domanik, for believing in this project, and helping me pay tribute to our good friend.

To all those friends and classmates with whom I shared the news of Manuel's passing, as well as wonderful reflections of our shared history, I thank-you from the bottom of my heart.

I wish to thank the wonderful team at Orange Hat, for being such a healthy and happy place to grow a book. I am very grateful to Shannon, for creating a context conducive to doing our best work, with substantial love and support. I also sing her praises for choosing such creative and dynamic and enthusiastic folks to be part of the team—a competent and caring crew.

I especially wish to thank Pam Parker, for an edit which gave the manuscript a sense of flow and focus. In the spirit of less is always more, she did wonders. Thanks for everything.

To Manuel, for being the kind of friend you only dream of having, and for being such a force of inspiration in my life, and for so many others.

It was an honor to have known you. Humility is a real rarity these days, but yours was genuine and effortless. I am glad to be able to pay tribute to your greatness. Like it or not, yes, I am getting the last word.

—Bill Grimbol

**Letter to me from Manuel when we were first discussing the possibility of this book.**

*Dear Bill—*

*Sign me up for the rafting trip. In fact, consider me officially launched. What a journey it will be. We didn't know it at the time, but we were sliding down the slippery river bank when we began exchanging some of our old writing pieces and talked on the phone more often than we have since Washington Junior High School. Those exchanges have been among the highlights of my retirement thus far. A natural progression will be for us to write a book of letters that capture formative events of our past and a bit of our future.*

*You bring your raft and I'll bring mine. I built my raft with the thick branches and trunks of trees that had roots in Racine, just like we did. We and the trees breathed the same air. The branches understand the* meaning of home and the significance of this trip. For this journey we will ride the same river, but pilot separate platforms to explore whatever river features reach out to grab our attention. Our letters will keep us connected during this journey as we share what we discover about ourselves and each other. We have been friends for almost sixty years. Still, I am prepared for surprises. You will surprise me. I will surprise you. We will surprise ourselves when we dig through layers of our histories.

You bring your eyes and I'll bring mine. We will need clear eyes, well-conditioned eyes, for all the looking back we will do, remembering the events that shaped the men we became. Some of my stories will be wrapped in scar tissue. Others will be wrapped in laughter, the arms of family members, the comfort of friends who shared our schools and streets, and the intimacy we had with the families we created as adults. When I retired after forty years of being a psychology professor, I lost my career, but I gained opportunities to remember. As a working professional, my life was all present and future. Each day my appointment book was full of events demanding immediate attention. I ate lunch sitting in front of my computer or during meetings. The rest of the time was used to plan the future--the next research steps, the next teaching module, the next paper, the next book chapter. Remembrance was an indulgence I could not afford. Now, I revel in looking back, particularly when I recall my life before progressive multiple sclerosis stole my ability to do the things that had brought me joy and spontaneity. I had muscles back then and optimism.

You bring your writing voice and I'll bring mine. You will tell me that Lake Michigan was created from blue sky and gray clouds. I will tell you that my grandfather and I pulled perch from the bottom of the lake and placed them in my memory where they are still swimming. I will feed off of your voice, especially when your words are like lyrics to songs *that need no additional melody. I expect that your voice will take me to church from time to time. I forgive you. I recognize that Pastor Bill needs to express himself on occasion even when his vestments are hanging in the office. I can't wait to read what we will write.*

*-Manuel*

*Manuel Barrera Jr.*

*William R. Grimbol*

**Reverend William Grimbol**

A gifted storyteller and preacher, Rev. William Grimbol has been a keynote speaker for school districts nationwide coping with the tragedy of adolescent suicide and depression.

He lives in Westminster, VT, with his son, Justin, daughter-in-law, Heather, and his grandson, James. He occasionally preaches and teaches, but mostly fills his days with reading, writing, and painting. The highlight of his days? Cartoon and cookie time with James. *Humility: The Key to Greatness* is Grimbol's eleventh published work.

www.ingramcontent.com/pod-product-compliance
Lightning Source LLC
LaVergne TN
LVHW031630070426
835507LV00025B/3417